A Traveller's Guide to
EARLY MEDIEVAL
BRITAIN

A Traveller's Guide to
EARLY MEDIEVAL
BRITAIN

Anthony Goodman & Michael Cyprien

HTI

Historical Times INC.
Harrisburg

CONTENTS

First published in 1986 by Historical Times Incorporated,
2245 Kohn Road, Harrisburg, PA 17105, USA
and by Routledge & Kegan Paul plc
11 New Fetter Lane, London EC4P 4EE and
29 West 35th Street, New York, NY 10001, USA

Text by Anthony Goodman
Photography and Art Direction by Michael Cyprien
Consultant Editor Dr Charles Kightly
Editorial Assistant Mary-Ann Smith
Filmset in England by BAS Printers Limited,
Over Wallop, Stockbridge, Hampshire
Printed in England by Balding + Mansell Limited
Wisbech, Cambridgeshire

Library of Congress Cataloging in Publication Data

Goodman, Anthony, 1936–
    A traveller's guide to early medieval Britain.
    (A Traveller's guide)
1. Great Britain—History—Medieval period, 1066–1485.
2. Great Britain—Antiquities—Guide-books.   3. Great
Britain—Description and travel—1971–   —Guide-books.
I. Cyprien, Michael.   II. Title.   III. Series.
DA175.G66 1986   914.1'04858   86–9790
ISBN 0-918678-16-1

British Library Cataloguing in Publication Data also available
ISBN 0 7102 0942 8

INTRODUCTION

One of the pleasures awaiting the traveller in search of memorials of the Middle Ages is to discover great buildings in one of the classic European styles. From the later twelfth century onwards the Gothic style in architecture spread through Britain. Its characteristics are tall piers and windows, clusters of shafts, pointed arches, criss-cross vaulting ribs, naturalistic sculptural detail and highly integrated schemes of design. Triumphs of Gothic achievement dating from our period are to be found in English cathedrals, abbeys and minsters – for instance, in Canterbury, Exeter, Lichfield and Lincoln Cathedrals, Westminster Abbey and York Minster. Perhaps the finest and certainly one of the most coherently designed Gothic cathedrals in Britain is Salisbury, begun on a new site in 1220.

Salisbury Cathedral was served in the Middle Ages by canons, but many British cathedrals were served by monks; their surviving buildings give good impressions of monastic life when it was at its medieval prime. Some other monastic churches survived the Reformation reasonably intact, because they were converted into cathedrals (for example, Bristol, Gloucester, Oxford, Peterborough); others became parish churches (Hexham, Tewkesbury). Extensive ruins of monastic churches built on a grand scale remain, especially those of the influential but isolationist Cistercian Order, which founded houses in remote valleys (for example Rievaulx). Monastic ruins in Scotland and Wales show receptivity to international trends in both ecclesiastical reform and architectural style: examples are Holyrood, Jedburgh and Sweetheart Abbeys in Scotland and Tintern Abbey in Wales. But Scottish and Welsh cathedrals were, in general, unpretentious in scale and design: exceptions being Glasgow and St Davids Cathedrals.

England is rich in the survival of buildings or ruins from our period associated with cathedral, abbey and minster churches – such as cloisters, chapter-houses, monks' and canons' residential quarters, bishops' palaces and precinct walls and gates. The cloisters and chapter-house at Salisbury are among the finest examples, begun in the 1260s: Southwell Minster's chapter-house has outstanding naturalistic sculpture. The Abbot's Kitchen at Glastonbury is built on a scale to cater for high living: the Bishop's Palace at Wells is a fairytale castle, with moat and battlemented walls. The gatehouse at Thornton Abbey is perhaps the most imposing of many lordly monastic gates. At Wells the residences and facilities built for the Vicars Choral, who performed the liturgies in the cathedral, constitute what has been described as the finest medieval street in Europe.

In the fourteenth century a distinctive English architectural style developed, in which the emphasis often found in English Gothic on horizontal as well as vertical lines culminated in trellis-work patterns. In this 'Perpendicular' style structure and decoration were fused to produce a strong linear effect. Early examples of Perpendicular are the reconstructed choir of Gloucester Cathedral and the rebuilt church at Edington. Fine fourteenth-century interiors in the style are the naves of Canterbury and Winchester Cathedrals. Perpendicular also features prominently in notable secular buildings of the period, such as the new domestic range at Berkeley Castle and the Great Hall of Penshurst Place. The recurrence of the Black Death from 1348 onwards did not dim architectural inspiration or the urge to build on a magnificent scale.

Throughout Britain Reformation iconoclasm was to wreak havoc on ecclesiastical figure sculpture – the survival of statues on the west fronts of Exeter and Wells Cathedrals is remarkable. The medieval interior furnishings of churches have often succumbed to changes of taste as well as usage. Few wall paintings survive like the astonishing ones at Claverley, or panel paintings such as the exquisite examples found at Thornham Parva. Nevertheless, many furnishings from our period still exist in English churches. There are imposing sets of choir stalls, mostly in cathedrals, furnished with misericords, hinged seats which gave some support to those standing through the long liturgies, on the underside of which are often found sacred and profane carvings, a gallery of medieval life.

The most spectacular examples of secular architecture are the castles built by kings and magnates, dominating their surroundings with the elaborate new stone fortifications which were replacing timber ones. The results of such transformations can be clearly seen at two of the most important English royal fortresses, the Tower of London and Dover Castle. Conisborough and Framlingham are examples of different types of baronial fortification, as are Bothwell and Dirleton in Scotland. Two other Scottish castles, Kildrummy and Rothesay, were respectively designed to advance royal and baronial power into the Highlands. In Wales, Pembroke and Caerphilly Castles mark stages in the encroachment of Anglo-Norman lords into the native principalities. The castles built by Edward I during and after his conquest of North Wales in the 1280s (of which Caernarvon, Conwy and Harlech are the most striking survivals) constitute one of the finest remaining medieval defence systems, a peak of achievement in the history of fortification.

Edward II's failure to control Scotland necessitated the fortification of the English Borders by their inhabitants, vulnerable to raids in the fourteenth century. They built solid, grim towers as residences or occasional refuges, such as that at Corbridge (where the parochial vicar could defend himself against marauding Scots) and the two towers which still dominate the centre of Hexham. Elsewhere in England the nobility were placing greater emphasis on the provision of domestic comfort. They had suites of separate apartments built, giving them privacy away from the busy communal life of the great hall and domestic offices. Longthorpe Tower and Ightham Mote are examples of nobles' residences which were essentially fortified country houses. Castles were for long to continue being built in England, but mainly as status symbols for peers and knights – Nunney Castle is a bijou Bastille. Successful merchants were also acquiring and improving country houses; Penshurst Place was renovated by a London merchant, Stokesay Castle by a provincial one.

The emergence of merchants as important groups in society resulted from the great expansion of towns and trade in the twelfth and thirteenth centuries. Urban expansion has left a lop-sided architectural legacy. Few secular city and town buildings survive – exceptions being wealthy "Jews' houses" at Bury St Edmunds and Lincoln, parts of the Mercers Company's hall at York, the city walls and gates there, and town walls at Caernavon, Conwy and Oxford. But many parish churches and fragments of monasteries and friaries remain, which were focusses of urban social life and public ceremony: and it is to these that the traveller needs to go for some flavour of town living in the period. Stamford has good examples of parish churches and Lincoln one of an early friary.

Little remains visible from this period, however, of the dwellings of the great majority of the population, the peasantry and urban poor. In most areas peasant housing was of a primitive and often flimsy nature, consisting of timber frameworks with an infilling of wattle (interlaced twigs and branches) and daub (plaster of mud and cowdung). Floors were of beaten earth and roofs thatched; there were no chimneys or glazed windows. Animals were often housed under the same roof as humans. The open-air museum at Singleton in Sussex gives some impressions of peasants' houses and way of life, through the re-erection and reconstruction of rural structures.

I owe thanks to the many authors whose work I have consulted. I have in particular been heavily dependent on Pevsner's *Buildings of England* series and on Department of the Environment guide books. I also owe thanks to Mr Kim Prior for information about the frescoes in Claverley Church and to Professor G. A. Shepperson for information about "Old Scarlett" in Peterborough Cathedral: and I have benefited much from Dr. Richard Rose's knowledge of medieval Carlisle and the Anglo-Scottish Borders.

Anthony Goodman, Edinburgh 1986

1 Acton Burnell
2 Alfriston Clergy
3 Arbroath Abbey
4 Aydon Castle
5 Beaumaris Castle
6 Belsay Castle
7 Berkeley Castle
8 Beverley
9 Boston
10 Bothwell Castle
11 Bradford-on-Avon
12 Bristol
13 Bury St Edmunds
14 Butley Priory
15 Caerlaverock Castle
16 Caernarvon Castle
17 Caerphilly Castle
18 Cambuskenneth Abbey
19 Canterbury
20 Carlisle
21 Carreg Cennen Castle
22 Chepstow Castle
23 Chipchase Castle
24 Claverley
25 Cobham
26 Coldingham Priory
27 Conisbrough Castle
28 Conwy Castle
29 Corbridge
30 Criccieth Castle
31 Crowland
32 Croxden Abbey
33 Direlton Castle
34 Dorchester-on-Thames
35 Dornoch Cathedral
36 Dover
37 Drum Castle
38 Dunkeld
39 Dunstaffnage Castle
40 Dustanburgh Castle
41 Edinburgh
42 Edington
43 Elsing
44 Exeter
45 Flint Castle
46 Framlingham
47 Geddington
48 Glasgow Cathedral
49 Glastonbury
50 Gloucester
51 Great Coxwell
52 Great Yarmouth
53 Haddon Hall
54 Harlech Castle
55 Hexham
56 Ightham Mote
57 Jedburgh
58 Kidwelly
59 Kildrummy
60 Langley Castle
61 Lichfield
62 Lincoln
63 London
64 Longthorpe Tower
65 Ludlow

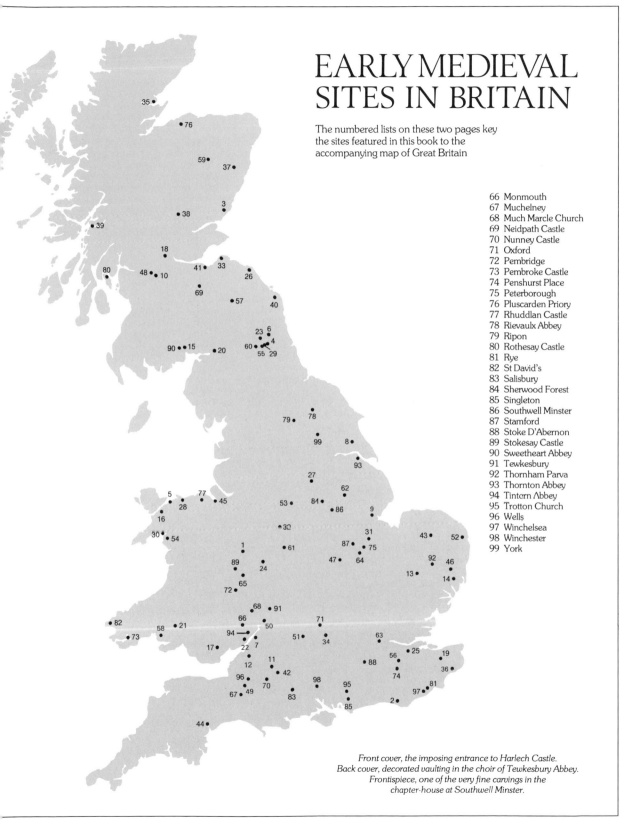

EARLY MEDIEVAL SITES IN BRITAIN

The numbered lists on these two pages key
the sites featured in this book to the
accompanying map of Great Britain

Front cover, the imposing entrance to Harlech Castle.
Back cover, decorated vaulting in the choir of Tewkesbury Abbey.
Frontispiece, one of the very fine carvings in the
chapter-house at Southwell Minster.

ACTON BURNELL Shropshire
OS 126 SJ 534019

The castle and church are eight miles south of historic Shrewsbury, on a minor road between the A49 towards Ludlow and the A458 towards Bridgnorth, and signposted from both. Not far to the south-west of the castle (and just off the A49) is the fascinating working farm museum at Acton Scott, and the picturesque hill country around Church Stretton.

Robert Burnell (d.1292) rose from the ranks of the minor provincial gentry to be the king's chancellor. He was the sort of hard-working, ambitious bureaucrat who remained approachable, generous and pleasure-loving. By 1260 he was employed by the Lord Edward (the future Edward I) and retained throughout his life the irascible king's confidence. Edward made him bishop of Bath and Wells in 1275. Burnell wanted to found a family fortune, and a pedigree was forged for him tracing his ancestry back to the Norman Conquest. At his death he held in part or in whole eighty-two manors in nineteen counties (twenty-one in Shropshire). He had acquired the whole manor of Acton Burnell, his birthplace, by 1269 and received royal licence to fortify in 1284.

Extensive ruins remain of the little castle which he had built there during the next few years. It is a rectangular block or tower-house, with rectangular towers projecting at the corners, four storeys in height. There are remains within of the great hall and chambers. The castle was not intended to withstand more than lightly armed attack, and it is in fact an early example of a fortification contrived as much for show as defence, a contrast with the

masterpieces of medieval military art which Edward was then having built in Wales. The castle and Burnell's other possessions were inherited by his nephew Philip: but the Burnell line died out in the fourteenth century. Succeeding manorial lords may have lived in the castle down to the seventeenth century. About one hundred yards east of it are the remains, principally stone gable ends, of a long, low medieval building, possibly a barn. This is traditionally said to have been the meeting-place of a parliament in 1283.

The parish church of St Mary, next to the castle, was probably rebuilt by the bishop: it has similar confidently sculpted decorative detail. The church is cruciform, and substantially unaltered, apart from the tower of 1887–89. It contains a late thirteenth-century font, a brass to Sir Nicholas Burnell (d.1382), and also tomb effigies of Sir Richard Lee (d.1591) and Sir Humphrey Lee (d.1632), the latter the work of Nicholas Stone. Sir Richard's actual helmet remains: it was customary to carry a knight's accoutrements in his funeral procession and hang them over his tomb. They have, however, disappeared from most churches.

ALFRISTON CLERGY HOUSE East Sussex
OS 199 TQ 521030

Alfriston village stands on the edge of the South Downs, three miles north-east of Seaford and about thirteen miles east of Brighton via the A27 and a minor road turning south at Berwick: cut on a hillside nearby is the huge prehistoric figure called the Long Man of Wilmington (544035).

The Clergy House dates from the fourteenth century. It is timber-framed and has a high and deeply overhanging thatched roof. In the Middle Ages the house was lived in by the clergy who ministered to the parish. From the end of the fourteenth century the right to appoint the vicars of Alfriston belonged to the Augustinian priory at Michelham, and canons from the priory may have been sent to serve here. Medieval clergy houses are fairly rare survivals: this one was quite imposing. It has a hall where the priests dined, with a crownpost roof and original timber frame, and a floor composed of rammed chalk sealed with sour milk. At one end is the solar

wing where the priests slept, and at the other the service wing where their servants lived and worked.

The parish church of St Andrew dates from the fourteenth century. In the village there are other fine timber-framed houses, such as the Ship Inn dating from the fifteenth century. This has exterior carvings, including one of St George and the Dragon on the sill of an oriel window. By the time this was carved, the cult of St George was the focus for English national sentiment; when the Holy Roman Emperor visited Henry V in 1416 he gave him an arm bone of the saint.

ARBROATH ABBEY Tayside
OS 54 NO 644413

Arbroath is on the north-east coast of Scotland and the A92, roughly seventeen miles north-east of Dundee: the abbey stands near the town centre. To the east of Arbroath a signposted Nature Trail follows a picturesque section of the rocky coastline.

Arbroath Abbey was founded in 1178 by William the Lion, King of Scots, after his release from three years' captivity in Normandy. He had been the prisoner of Henry II of England, whose realm he had unsuccessfully invaded. William founded the abbey in honour of his old friend St Thomas Becket, whose martyrdom in Canterbury Cathedral was depicted on its seal. The monks whom the king brought to Arbroath were Tironensians, members of a reformed French Benedictine Order founded by St Bernard of Tiron, and it seems likely that he had become familiar with the Order while he was in Normandy. He endowed the house lavishly – its property included the burgh of Arbroath: and by 1214, when William died, the building of the abbey church was sufficiently advanced to allow his burial before the High Altar. In 1816 a coffin

containing human bones was found in the choir, above which was a headless civilian effigy. This may have been the king's tomb.

The church was completed by 1233, and Arbroath Abbey was to become a Scottish national shrine. For in its chapter house, on April the sixth 1320, the assembled Scots nobility sealed the famous "Declaration of Arbroath", a letter to the Pope supporting King Robert the Bruce and proclaiming their independence from English rule. So when daring Scots patriots removed the "Stone of Destiny" from Westminster Abbey on Christmas Eve 1950 – thus reclaiming the ancient coronation stone of the Scots kings, stolen from Scone by Edward I during the Wars of Independence – it was to Arbroath that they chose to bring it, leaving it on the site of the abbey's high altar on April the eleventh 1951.

The buildings of Arbroath Abbey have been extensively plundered by the folk of the burgh, but the ruins, in dramatic red sandstone, give an impression of its former magnificence. Of the church consecrated in 1233, there remain substantial fragments of the east end, the south transept, the south wall of the nave and the western towers on either side of the great rose window. Most of the monastic buildings have disappeared, but their foundations have been excavated. The most substantial survivals are the abbot's house, dating partly from the earliest phase of building works and partly from the fifteenth century: and the imposing gatehouse range, extending from the south-east corner of the church. This dates mainly from the late thirteenth and early fourteenth centuries.

Arbroath is a pleasant seaside resort and fishing port. The curing of haddock is a domestic industry, producing a local delicacy, "Arbroath smokies".

Aydon Castle stands on a rise surrounded on three of its five sides by the Aydon Burn. It consists of a small inner bailey in the south-east corner of an outer bailey, and it illustrates how some Northumberland gentry were aspiring to live in style at the end of the thirteenth century, as well as the measures they took to protect their properties in the less secure frontier conditions of the next hundred years. The nucleus of the castle is a late thirteenth century hall-house which forms the southern range of the inner bailey. This impressive battlemented block, with well-preserved interior features, comprises a first floor hall, with a cruciform private wing to the east of it, and service quarters to the west. But in the early fourteenth century a new kitchen was built as an extension along the west side of the inner bailey, and its two remaining sides were enclosed by a stone wall. In the same century the outer bailey was also enclosed in stone.

The building of the hall-house has been attributed to Robert Reymes (d.1323), as has the fortification of the inner bailey – he procured a licence to fortify his house in 1305. He was heavily involved in Edward I's Scottish wars, especially in the service of Sir Henry Percy, a rising star in Scotland and Northumberland. In 1316 Reymes successfully petitioned Edward II for compensation for his losses of horses, armour and other goods in the Scottish wars, the costs of his ransom after having been taken prisoner, and the waste in his properties caused by Scottish pillaging. A raiding party had captured his castle the previous year. Nevertheless, considering the continued occupancy of Aydon by the Reymes family and their efforts to strengthen it, it is likely that he had made some compensatory profits of war – and benefited financially from the support he gave to the Percies. Thus Border conditions created close ties between magnates and gentry.

In 1346 the castle was surrendered to King David II of Scotland during the disastrous invasion which ended with his capture at the battle of Neville's Cross near Durham – a victory which gave long-term security to the English Borderers. In 1450 the castle was said to be ruinous – the Reymes family presumably having moved out: and in 1541 it was acquired by the Carnabys of Hexham, who lived there and made renovations.

AYDON CASTLE
Northumberland
OS 87 NZ 002664
The castle is some sixteen miles west of Newcastle-upon-Tyne (via the A69) and one and a half miles north of Corbridge (with its fine church and Vicar's pele) via the B6321 and a minor road turning west just beyond Aydon village. About a mile to the north of the castle is another well-preserved medieval tower-house, Halton Castle, and the line of Hadrian's Wall, with its numerous Roman remains.

Beaumaris Castle was the last of the great fortresses built by Edward I to hold down North Wales. Its foundation, with an adjoining English borough, was in response to the revolt in 1294 of Madoc ap Llywelyn. The castle was built substantially in the years 1295–98: the architect was James of St George, and arguably it is his masterpiece. Further work was done in 1306–13, but the castle appears never to have been completed: many of the towers were never properly roofed.

The site chosen was a low, marshy one on the seashore: so that Beaumaris lacks the spectacular setting of some Edwardian castles. It consists of two concentric lines of fortification, forming the inner and outer baileys. The rectangular inner bailey has drum towers at the corners, stirrup-shaped towers in the middle of the east and west sides, and double-towered gatehouses in the middle of the north and south sides. The gatehouses had two doors and three portcullises each, and the south gatehouse also had

BEAUMARIS CASTLE
Anglesey, Gwynedd
OS 115 SH 608763
Beaumaris is on the south-east coast of Anglesey, some seven miles north of Bangor and the Menai Bridge from the Welsh mainland. Edward I's contemporary fortresses of Conwy and Caernarvon are both relatively close, and all three castles can be visited in one longish day.

The towers of the north gatehouse rise above the castle's outer curtain wall.

9

a small barbican. Both gatehouses could additionally be defended from attack from the rear: the north one (the last resort) could be isolated from the wall walk running round the inner bailey. The tower in the middle of the west side houses a chapel on the first floor, which has a vaulted, lime-washed ceiling and panelled walls with lancet windows.

The defences of the inner bailey entirely dwarf those of the outer bailey that encompasses it. This is octagonal in shape, almost completely moated, and has its north and south gates built carefully out of alignment with those of the inner bailey. If besiegers broke through an outer gate, therefore, they would have to dash for the inner gate down an alley of fire – some of it possibly still coming from the outer wall, and now directed inward. The south gate of the outer bailey was extended parallel to a fortified projection across the moat, Gunner's Walk. The gate and the walk formed a dock, allowing an arm of the sea to lap the castle wall. In time of siege, a ship could thus slip into dock under the protection of fire from the parapets of the watergate and Gunner's Walk.

The walls of the borough no longer survive, but noteworthy buildings in the town are the parish church of St Mary and St Nicholas (fourteenth century), the Bull's Head (1472) and County Hall (seventeenth century).

The north-west corner of moated Beaumaris Castle.

BELSAY CASTLE
Northumberland
OS 88 NZ 088785
Belsay is fourteen miles north-west of Newcastle-upon-Tyne, via the A696 (from which it is signposted): the castle forms a delightful group with a ruined seventeenth century mansion and a complete neo-Classical house of 1810–17, all set in landscaped gardens. It is open from April to September only.

The tower at Belsay appears in a list of fortifications in Northumberland made in 1415 – it then belonged to Sir John Middleton, one of the shire's leading gentlefolk, who sat for Northumberland in parliament in 1417 and was its sheriff in 1423. The tower may have been built in the first half of the fourteenth century. At that time, in less disturbed parts of England, noble families often lived in manor houses which were only lightly defended by a moat or precinct wall: but at Belsay (as elsewhere in the troubled Borders), the gentry retreated into self-contained tower-houses (often free standing) reminiscent of Norman keeps. At Belsay the walls are of great thickness, and the hall and private quarters were (for security) in the upper storeys. The most striking exterior feature is the concentration of defence works at the top of the walls – there are battlements, overhanging machicolations and little projecting turrets at the four corners.

Peasant farmers as well as gentlefolk in Northumberland apparently built defensive towers – though these are likely to have been simpler than the tower at Belsay, and were sometimes used as temporary refuges, like air-raid shelters. In 1435 an Italian diplomat, Aeneas Sylvius Piccolomini (the future Pope Pius II) spent a night at a Northumberland farmhouse. He describes how the local priest, the host, the men and the children took refuge for the night in a tower a long way off, for fear of the Scots who were accustomed to make raids across the river Tweed. The terrified Aeneas was left at the farmhouse, as were the womenfolk, who made a circle round the fire and cleaned hemp all night. Aeneas gives a vivid picture of an insecure society, but one which had adapted to frontier conditions.

BERKELEY CASTLE
Gloucestershire
OS 162 ST 685989
Berkeley is twenty-four miles north of Bristol and about the same distance south of Gloucester, just west of the A38 Bristol-Gloucester road: it can also be reached via the M5 motorway, either via exit 13 and the A38 south or exit 14 and A38 north. The castle is open from April until September.

Cannon greet the visitor at Berkeley Castle.

This castle, remarkably, is still lived in by the direct descendants of the man who rebuilt its defences in the twelfth century – the Berkeleys. A motte and bailey castle was constructed here by William the Conqueror's supporter William Fitz Osbern, to command the Vale of Berkeley, a route northwards from Bristol between the Severn estuary and the Cotswold Hills to the important strategic junction of Gloucester. Fitz Osbern's descendants supported King Stephen in the civil wars of his reign; and Stephen's opponent and successor, the victorious Henry II, gave the castle to his own supporter Robert Fitz Harding, reeve of Bristol and ancestor of the Berkeleys. Fitz Harding levelled the motte downwards and enclosed it with a "shell keep", which remains substantially unaltered, except for the fourteenth century insertions of the Thorpe Tower and the gatehouse.

In 1327 the deposed Edward II was imprisoned in the keep: and when fumes from carrion in the basement failed to kill him, he is said to have been horribly murdered here. The owner of the castle, Thomas Lord Berkeley, prudently stayed away during Edward's imprisonment. It was this Berkeley who rebuilt the bailey – allegedly with the profits which he gained in Edward III's wars in France. His great hall, chapel (with painted ceiling), kitchen and private apartments, though altered by continuous occupation, give a good impression of the living standards of a great noble of the period. The subsequent history of the castle has been uneventful, except during the Civil War, when it fortunately escaped essentially unscathed from a brief siege and dismantling.

The parish church of St Mary has restored thirteenth-century wall paintings, and an early fourteenth-century Easter Sepulchre on the north side of the chancel. Its fifteenth-century Berkeley Chapel contains some magnificent tombs of the Berkeleys, including that of Thomas Lord Berkeley (d.1361), the rebuilder of the castle.

There was a monastery here in the early eighth century, to which St John of Beverley, Bishop successively of Hexham and York (d.721), retired. He was buried there and his tomb became a cult centre – which helps to account for the determination and ability of the canons who served Beverley Minster to rebuild the church on an impressive scale. Opportunities to do so arose from the disasters which befell it: in 1188 it was badly damaged in a fire and, when the pre-Conquest tower was heightened (c.1213), it collapsed. So between 1220 and c.1260 a major rebuilding was undertaken, and the present choir and greater and lesser transepts date from this period. In the triforia and clerestories dark Purbeck marble contrasts elegantly with white West Yorkshire limestone. Here is Gothic in its first full flowering, with tall pillars, deep-cut arcade moulds and

a pattern of intersecting vault ribs complementing the pointed arches of the three-tiered arcades. The finely carved reredos is fourteenth century work restored in the nineteenth, and there are four elaborately canopied wooden sedilia dating from the later fourteenth century to the south of the sanctuary. The choir has sixty-eight stalls with misericords dating from the early sixteenth century.

Work on a new nave, echoing the design patterns of the east end, was begun by 1308. In the period 1390–1420 the west end, the twin-towered west front, and the north porch were completed. The west towers and front comprise a fine essay in the Perpendicular style, imposing and elegant: they are visible from afar in this level East Yorkshire countryside.

Beverley Minster has a profusion of figure

BEVERLEY Humberside
OS 107 TA 037393
The ancient and attractive town of Beverley is some eight miles north of Hull, via the A1174; and about thirty-five miles east of York via the A1079 over the Wolds. The walk from the North Bar and St Mary's church (via the market place) to the Minster and Friary is rewarding architecturally, and Beverley also has an interesting new museum of military transport (signposted from the Minster).

The unique medieval staircase which led to the chapter-house before its demolition in 1550, seen from within the choir.

sculpture, notably the minstrels and musicians sculpted on the corbels of the nave pillars. Most remarkable of all, however, are the figure of angels, knights, beasts, fruit and leaves carved on the great stone canopy over the plain-topped tomb to the north of the sanctuary – apparently the tomb of Idoine Clifford (d.1365), wife of Henry second Lord Percy. The Percies, great landowners in the East Riding of Yorkshire and often involved in Beverley affairs, were then rising stars, soon to attain an earldom. Joan Evans considered this monument "one of the most beautiful creations of the English middle ages": at its apex God receives the soul of the deceased lady, and angels hold the instruments of the Passion. In a chapel at the east end is the rather plain tomb of an enigmatic Percy – Henry, fourth earl of Northumberland (d.1489), who was mysteriously killed by a mob of Yorkshiremen. He had been restored to the earldom by Edward IV in 1470, and had co-operated with Edward's brother Richard in the north when the latter was Duke of Gloucester, then when he was king. But at Bosworth in 1485 his troops remained passive whilst Richard III was defeated and killed. One well-informed contemporary says the earl had an understanding with Henry Tudor (they had known one another as boys): so perhaps after Bosworth the earl was a marked man in the north.

Beverley remains essentially a medieval town. It had good land communications in the Middle Ages with York and the leading port of Hull and may have already been a weaving centre when its lords, the Archbishops of York, gave it privileges in the early twelfth century, confirmed by the Crown. Beverley merchants were among leading

exporters of Yorkshire wool at the end of the thirteenth century. Their wealth and aspirations are reflected in the parish church of St Mary near the opposite end of the medieval town from the minster – and mounting an elegant challenge to it in magnificence, if not in scale. Beverley, indeed, would be worth a visit for its parish church alone. The twelfth century church has almost disappeared through subsequent medieval alterations and enlargements, particularly to accommodate the chapels of the town gilds: and what we now see dates mainly from the fourteenth to sixteenth centuries. Above St Michael's Chapel, dating from the second quarter of the fourteenth century, are rooms where the priests who served the altars in the chapels lived. Together with the minster, the church has what is believed to be the largest collection anywhere of carvings of medieval musi-

cians and their instruments (some 140 in all). This was because the gild of northern minstrels met in the town. There are other notable figure carvings in the church, such as the grimacing Beverley Imp (doorway leading to the staircase in the north-east corner of the chancel), the elephant with howdah (stall misericord), and the pilgrim rabbit (doorway to the sacristy). Beverley saw a lot of pilgrims, passing through to the shrine of St William at York as well as coming to that of St John in the minster.

Near St Mary's church is the North Bar, the only one of the town gates to survive. Dating from 1409, it is remarkable as an early example of medieval brickwork. The restored medieval Friary (now a youth hostel) is near the minster, and also well worth a visit.

The Percy Tomb, one of the finest examples of medieval stone-carving to be seen in the country. Above, the north aisle from the east end.

The choir screen and organ at Beverley Minster are nineteenth and eighteenth century additions which blend harmoniously with their medieval setting.

BOSTON Lincolnshire
OS 131 TF 328442

About thirty-five miles south-east of Lincoln (via the A15, A17 and A1121) Boston can also be reached from the A1 via Grantham (with its notable church) and Sleaford. Set amid dead-flat Fenland, Boston's "Stump" is visible for miles around. Ten miles north-east of the town, via the B1183, B184 and B1192 (through New York!) is Tattershall Castle and church, two unusual medieval buildings well worth a visit.

The soaring tower of St Botolph's. Above, the richly carved choir – the misericords here are particularly fine examples of the craft.

Medieval Boston was administered as a subordinate manor of the earldom of Richmond, but in 1377 it was the tenth most populous town in England. Situated on the river Witham, it was the outport of Lincoln, thirty miles upstream, and was at the head of a complex of navigable waterways stretching into the Midlands. By the beginning of the thirteenth century it was among the leading centres of English overseas trade. Its annual St Botolph's Fair was one of the largest in the realm, a cosmopolitan meeting-place for the export of native wool and the import of Flemish cloth, Gascon wine and Norwegian dried fish (stockfish). The Hanse (the trading association of northern and western German merchants) had a Kontor (a trading post) permanently at Boston. By 1400, however, alien traders had almost disappeared from the town, and its fair had declined. Yet cloth continued to be exported and dyestuffs imported, and Boston remained an important centre of regional trade.

The Bostonians, lacking fully fledged urban institutions, expressed their civic pride in the building of the parish church of St Botolph. This has the tallest tower of any medieval English parish church, known as "the Stump". It soars up 272 feet high, over the muddy banks of the Witham. But its height had a practical purpose, for the top two storeys are open lanterns: the Stump was a lighthouse, guiding ships at sea and wayfarers over the Fenlands. The whole church is a rebuilding of the fourteenth and fifteenth centuries. Beneath the misericord seats of the choir stalls (c.1390) are homely carvings, and there are brasses and tomb effigies – notably that of the Hanseatic merchant Wissel Smalenburg of Münster (d.1340), who has a marble slab plainly incised with his praying figure.

The town also has fine eighteenth and nineteenth century buildings. Blackfriars Hall in Spain Lane was part of the Dominican friary, and the Guildhall dates from the fifteenth century: it is now the Borough Museum. In its cells the Pilgrim Fathers were imprisoned in 1607 after attempting to sail to America. Adjacent is Fydell House, built in 1726, which has an American Room set aside for the use of visitors from Boston, U.S.A.

15

Magna Carta and the Beginnings of Parliament

Magna Carta was the "great charter" issued to appease a baronial rebellion against King John in June 1215. The original draft of the charter has not survived, though in the British Library, London, there is a piece of parchment recording the "Articles of the Barons" on which the charter was based: John had his seal attached to this copy of the "Articles" at Runnymede, a field beside the river Thames between his castle at Windsor and the rebel barons' camp at Staines. Four copies survive of the charter, sent out from the royal chancery after the original had been sealed: two are in the British Library, the other two being at Lincoln and Salisbury Cathedrals.

Magna Carta was not the first general charter of privileges issued by a king since the Norman Conquest, promising that the Crown would govern in accordance with what public opinion in the realm considered to be fair and legitimate rules. Nor does it lack parallels in other parts of early medieval Europe. So it is not unique. But it is remarkable for its detail and comprehensiveness, as well as for its attempts to establish the rights of the "community of the realm" and of the individual, not just of an aristocratic elite. Its final clauses set up a novel and controversial constitutional device – a baronial council with powers to enforce the charter by coercing the king.

In fact, John found the whole business hard to stomach: and he regarded the issue of the charter as merely a tactical move to win friends and divide enemies. He also set to work to undo it; and within a few months Pope Innocent III had declared it null and void. Civil war was then renewed, being intensified in 1216 by the invasion of the French king's son Louis, an ally of the barons. But in October John unexpectedly died: and to rally support for his son Henry III, aged nine, the royalists reissued the charter shorn of its coercive clauses. Issues of the charter thereafter became a means for kings to reassure and appease angry subjects suspicious that the monarchy was acting high-handedly: Henry III re-issued it five more times, and Edward I repeated the process in 1297. From then onwards it always headed lists of the "statutes of the realm"; new kings always confirmed it. Magna Carta had come to symbolise the concept that England had a constitutional monarchy, whose role was to protect and not to abuse the liberties of subjects.

Edward I (1272–1307) was the first king who regularly summoned representatives of the shire communities and boroughs (called knights of the shires and burgesses) to attend some of the formal, often twice yearly, meetings he held with his leading officials, judges and most important subjects. These councils were beginning to be called "parliaments" in the thirteenth century. There was some advantage to communities in sending representatives to the king's council, though their expenses had to be paid: for it facilitated the bringing of local grievances about the behaviour of royal officials and others to the attention of the king and his chief ministers. Edward probably had this in mind, though his principal purpose was to bind the communities represented to obey and carry out decisions made in parliament about raising subsidies, going to war, punishing traitors and modifying laws. Edward I certainly did not intend the shire knights and burgesses to have a share in law-making or policy decisions. They were merely to petition, to listen and give their assent. But during the reign of Edward III (1327–77) there was a rapid and decisive evolution of parliamentary institutions. The Lords were emerging as a chamber with distinct roles in law-making and in making legal judgements, composed of bishops, abbots and of a developing hierarchy of secular peers. Shire knights and burgesses had meanwhile coalesced into a single chamber, the Commons, which established increasing control over the terms on which subsidies were granted, and whose petitions on matters of public concern, Edward III and his successors came to treat with great respect. The financial needs of kings (especially in time of war), the wealth and local power of gentry and merchants, and the way in which they came together as a nationwide force in parliament, all combined to give the Commons political leverage. This was especially noticeable to contemporaries at a parliament in 1376, which they called the Good Parliament. The ageing Edward III was neglecting affairs of state, drinking heavily and spending his time with a widely disliked mistress, Alice Perrers, who scandalously produced babies presumably fathered by the king. The Commons in parliament, unified in aim after stormy debates, took it upon themselves to reform the king's government, impeaching financial speculators and petitioning for the appointment of new councillors. They had a measure of success as a result of the king's illness, and sympathies in the Lords with their aims. The Commons of 1376, were not trying to arrogate power, or to alter their constitutional role. But they demonstrated that the representative element in parliament could act as a powerful force, which kings had to hear, manage and appease.

BOTHWELL CASTLE
Strathclyde
OS 64 NS 688594
The castle is set in parkland on the banks of the Clyde, seven miles south-east of Glasgow city centre via the M8, M73 and M74: leave the M74 at exit 5, signposted Bothwell, and drive north through Bothwell town; the castle is signposted to the west.

The castle may have been first built in stone by the Moray family in the second half of the thirteenth century. When Edward I invaded Scotland and deposed John Balliol from the kingship in 1296, an English garrison was installed. But in 1300, after a siege of fourteen months, the Scots stormed the castle. This stung Edward. In 1301 he besieged the castle in person, having a great siege-engine called "le berefrey" (the belfry) specially constructed at Glasgow – a great wooden tower to be wheeled laboriously up to the walls and from whose summit they could be directly assaulted. The garrison prudently surrendered, and Edward granted the castle and barony of Bothwell to Aymer de Valence, Earl of Pembroke. The English were still holding the castle in 1314 when Edward II was decisively defeated by Robert I at Bannockburn, and English fugitives from the battle sought refuge in the castle, which soon surrendered to Robert's brother Edward Bruce. The castle was then dismantled, but in 1336, when the young Edward III resumed dynastic intervention in Scotland, it was again occupied by the English, and was Edward's headquarters for part of that year. In 1337 Sir Andrew Moray, Regent of Scotland for David II, recaptured the castle, which was yet again rendered indefensible. In about 1362 the lordship came into the hands of Archibald the Grim, the Douglas lord of Gal-

loway. He restored the castle, and founded the collegiate church at Bothwell (the chancel of which remains), where he was buried in 1400.

The castle is sited in a bend of the river Clyde, on rocky ground which slopes steeply down to the river on two sides: a ditch was dug to protect the other sides. There is a rectangular inner bailey; beyond this was an outer bailey, of whose stone defences only foundations remain. At the west end of the inner bailey is the ruin of a remarkable thirteenth-century defence work, a huge keep which was circular on the outside and surrounded by its own moat: this keep could be defended independently from the rest of the castle. It was entered via a drawbridge from the inner bailey, the entrance being commanded by the north-west curtain wall. It may have been to tackle this keep – probably one of the most formidable fortifications that the much-travelled Edward I had encountered – that he had "le berefrey" constructed. The keep has been shattered – probably by the Scots when they recovered the castle in 1314. Most of the existing defences of the inner bailey, and the hall range at its eastern end, were constructed by the Douglases in the later fourteenth and early fifteenth centuries.
See **Flint**

BRADFORD-ON-AVON
Wiltshire
OS 173 ST 824604
Bradford-on-Avon is some seven miles south-east of Bath, via the A4 and A363: its barn and granary are to the south of the town centre.

A prosperous centre of cloth production during the later Middle Ages, Bradford-on-Avon is perhaps best known for its exquisite and miraculously well-preserved Anglo-Saxon church, only recognised as such in 1856. Yet it also contains another notable group of

buildings, once the property of the nuns of Shaftesbury who owned the town from 1001 until the Reformation. These are the great fourteenth century barn, some 168 feet long and equipped with a fine timber roof; and its adjacent two-storey stone granary.

BRISTOL Avon
OS 172 ST 590730
Bristol is 115 miles west of London, via the M4 motorway. The buildings described are all relatively close together in the city centre, in the area round the Floating Harbour: here too (near St Nicholas's church) is Corn Street, with its "Nail" pillars for bargaining (the origin of "cash on the nail") and the restored Victorian ship the S.S. Great Britain. Bristol makes a good centre for visits to sites in Gloucestershire, Somerset and (via the Severn Bridge) South Wales.

Medieval Bristol occupied a strong defensive site, almost surrounded by the river Avon and its tributary the Frome: the great royal castle (of which only fragments remain) gave protection where the natural water defences were weak. It was also well-placed as a centre for overseas trade, with easy access to rich hinterlands and for ships on the high tides funnelling up the Avon gorge. In the reign of Stephen (d.1154), indeed, Bristol was described as "nearly the richest of all the cities of the country, receiving merchandise by sailing vessels from foreign countries, placed in the most fruitful part of England, and by the very situation of the place the best defended of all the cities of England". During the 1180s the townsmen were dealing in cloth, wool, leather and corn, and by the end of the fourteenth century Bristol had expanded beyond its stone walls and water defences: stretching as far as Temple Meads was the new industrial suburb, whose cloth production had made Bristol one of the principal English manufacturing centres.

Wartime bombing and post-war development have destroyed much of what remained of the medieval city. But there are still a large number of churches with medieval features, notably the originally Norman St Nicholas; the fourteenth century St John the Baptist; the ruined Temple Church (to which the medieval weavers added their chapel); and the imposing later medieval St Mary Redcliffe, described by Elizabeth I as "the fairest, goodliest and most famous parish church in England". This last church, especially, is a reflection of the wealth and enterprise of Bristol merchants.

The largest surviving group of medieval buildings in Bristol, however, are at College Green, on a hill which in the Middle Ages was just outside the city, to the west across the river Frome. Here, on or near a reputedly ancient Christian site, Robert Fitz Harding founded St Augustine's Abbey, a house of Augustinian canons, in the 1140s – he later retired to become a canon there. The church (now a cathedral) was dedicated in c.1170,

and the main remnant is the elaborately decorated chapter-house: but the church is
chiefly remarkable for the eastern parts
rebuilt in the first half of the fourteenth century, which exhibit a startling originality of
design. This originality is also apparent in
what became the Berkeley Chapel, south of
the south choir aisle: the church has several
tombs and effigies of the Berkeleys of
Berkeley Castle. The south transept was completed and the crossing tower and the north
transept rebuilt c.1470–1515; while choir
stalls, with a fine set of misericord carvings,
date from 1520. There are some remains of
conventual buildings. The church received
cathedral status in 1542.

On the other side of the College Green is
the Lord Mayor's Chapel. This was part of
an almonry founded by Maurice de Gaunt
(d.1230), grandson of Robert Fitz Harding:
there was to be a permanent chaplain, one
hundred poor people were to be clothed
each day and the foundation was to be
supervised by St Augustine's Abbey. Gaunt's
nephew Robert de Gournay, however,
refounded the charity as an independent
hospice with a master, four chaplains, eight
clerks and twelve poor folk.

The small cruciform chapel, therefore, is
an unusual survival from an early charitable
foundation. The existing nave and transepts
were begun in c.1230, the southern aisle
dates from c.1270, and two chantry chapels
were added in the early sixteenth century. In
the south aisle chapel are monuments, with
mailed effigies, of the two founders, Gaunt
and Gournay, and there also fine tomb effigies of Sir Maurice Berkeley of Uley (d.1464)
and his wife Ellen. Berkeley wears a collar
of suns and roses, the livery badges of
Edward IV.
See **Berkeley**

The south aisle, looking towards the east end of the cathedral.

An elaborate example of medieval stone carving in Bristol Cathedral's Lady Chapel.

BURY ST EDMUNDS Suffolk
OS 155 TL 856650

Bury St Edmunds, one of the most interesting historic towns in East Anglia, is twenty-eight miles east of Cambridge via the A45. The abbey remains are at the east end of the town centre (TL 858642), the Great Gate being in Abbeygate Street, the Guildhall opposite in Guildhall Street, and Moyses Hall nearby in Cornhill. St Mary's church is worth visiting for the tomb of John Baret (d.1467) and the mirrored ceiling above it.

King Edmund of East Anglia was martyred in 870 by Danes who had invaded England and overrun his kingdom. In 1020 Cnut, the Danish warleader who had become Christian king of the English, endowed a Benedictine monastery to honour St Edmund and house his shrine. The saint and his monastery were to be especially revered by English kings (he is figured on the Wilton Diptych, an exquisite fourteenth-century altar painting honouring Richard II, now in the National Gallery, London). Lands and other gifts were lavished on the monastery by pilgrims, making it one of the wealthiest in England, and the surrounding region constituted the "liberty of St Edmund", ruled by the abbot's officials, not the king's. In the century or so after the Norman Conquest, the abbey church was rebuilt on a magnificent scale, but only pathetic fragments remain. By the thirteenth century the town at the abbey gates had expanded: it was to participate in the growth of the East Anglian cloth industry, in what became by the early sixteenth century one of the most prosperous regions of the realm.

Since the abbey kept a tight control over the town's affairs, relations between monks and townsmen were already bad in the thirteenth century, and in 1327 the townsfolk revolted. Soon after this, work was started on the abbey's defensive Great Gatehouse, still standing. Its main facade is an elaborate, coherent composition. Tall niches and parallel arcades give it an engaging spikiness, balanced by four large roundels and the high curve of the gateway arch. During the Peasants' Revolt in 1381 the townsmen called in a brutal band of rebels led by a renegade cleric, John Wrawe, to intimidate the monks. This band slew the prior and another monk. When the Revolt was suppressed, however, the monks were back in the saddle, and remained there till Henry VIII dissolved their house. The ancient local resentment against them may have added to the thoroughness with which the monastic buildings were subsequently robbed of their stone and the only intact fragment is the Norman Gate.

Two medieval parish churches in the town are worth visiting—St Mary's and St James's (the latter being now the cathedral). Moyses Hall, in the Butter market, is an early example of an urban stone dwelling, dating from the twelfth century. It has been suggested that it may have been a Jewish house or a synagogue. The Guildhall is essentially a fifteenth century structure, while the Abbot's Bridge over the river Lark dates from the thirteenth century.

The isolated hamlet of Butley is eighteen miles east of Ipswich, via the A12 to Woodbridge, the A1152, and the B1084 through Rendlesham Forest. Three miles to the east, near the coast, is Orford Castle with its unusual polygonal keep: and Framlingham Castle is some ten miles to the north west.

The richly decorated south front of the priory gatehouse.

Butley Priory was founded in 1171 by Ranulph Glanvill, a chief justiciar and leading official of Henry II. A famous treatise on English law is attributed to him: even if he did not write it, the fact that the attribution was made demonstrates his high reputation as a lawyer. In the heroic style of the age, he was as much at ease on a warhorse as behind a desk. He captured the king of Scots at the battle of Alnwick (1174) and died while accompanying Richard I on crusade. The endowments which his priory was to receive made it one of the richest houses of its Order in England.

The only part still substantially standing is the gatehouse (c.1320–25), one of a number of imposing monastic gatehouses erected in the fourteenth and fifteenth centuries which look like secular buildings. They may have reflected a need felt by monks, at a time when monastic ideals were sometimes attacked or not appreciated, to proclaim the stability of their house and to make it appear more congenial to visiting local nobles. At Butley there is a large central block with side towers. Above the gateway, which has separate entrances for carriages and pedestrians, is a window and niches for statues. But between the top of the gateway and these features are five rows of heraldic shields in a chequered design. These introduce us to something of the world known to the Augustinin canons, distant and local. In the top row are the shields of the Holy Roman Empire, France, St Edmund (whose cult was the focus for East Anglian patriotism); the symbols of Christ's Passion, England, Leon and Castile – and the local family of Huntshelve, in such exalted company doubtless because of connections with the priory. In the lower rows are the shields of earls, then of prominent barons, then of local knightly families. The secular heraldry mingling with the religious symbolism reflects the canons' view of themselves and their house as having strong links with secular society, besides belonging to an Order – sentiments of which the Monk in Chaucer's *Canterbury Tales* might have approved. *See* **Bury St Edmunds**

A chequer-board pattern of heraldic shields at Butley Priory.

Massive supports butress the structure of the gatehouse.

This magnificent triangular castle was probably begun during the 1270s, shortly before the long struggle between Edward I of England and the Scots: sited on low marshy ground within sight of the Solway Firth, it may have been originally intended either to guard the Dumfriesshire coastal plain or to act as a bridgehead for English landings. In 1300 Edward himself came to besiege it, and a contemporary poem written about this event both emphasises Caerlaverock's natural defences and describes the castle graphically: "in shape it was like a shield, for it had but three sides round it, with a tower at each corner; but one of them was a double one, so high, so long and so wide that the gate was beneath it, well made and strong, with a drawbridge and a sufficiency of other defences".

Caerlaverock fell on that occasion, and it was to change hands several times – either by assault or by treachery – during the almost incessant Anglo-Scottish warfare of the next three hundred years, at least once suffering partial demolition in the process. The only substantial parts of the present building which date from around 1300, indeed, are sections of the gatehouse, the west wall, and the south tower. The rest of the fortress was rebuilt during the later Middle Ages by the Maxwell family, who held Caerlaverock from the fifteenth to the seventeenth century, and who also added wide-mouthed gun ports to its

CAERLAVEROCK CASTLE
Dumfries and Galloway
OS 84 NY 026656
The castle is six miles south-east of Dumfries, on the B725; the area around it is a bird sanctuary for the waders and wildfowl of the Solway Firth.

gatehouse in about 1593. Later still (after peace had descended on the Borders with the union of the English and Scottish crowns under James VI and I) Robert Maxwell, Earl of Nithsdale, built the extraordinary mansion within the castle courtyard: begun in 1634 and still in good order, "Nithsdale's Apartments" confront the traveller who passes through the medieval gateway with the spirit of the Scottish Renaissance. The peaceful times, however, were not to last long: for in 1640 Caerlaverock fell to a final siege by a Covenanting army, and this time it was not restored.

23

The Noble Way of Life

A fundamental distinction between the medieval noble and commoner was that the former did not earn his living by menial tasks, soiling his hands. In the romances which became the leisure reading of the nobility in the thirteenth century the whiteness of ladies' complexions and hands is praised – a sign that they were not exposed to the elements like common women, who grew weatherbeaten or sunburnt working in the fields. Noblemen were noted as being characteristically taller and of finer physique than others – a phenomenon probably deriving from better living conditions, a more assured diet, and accommodation in stone buildings with tiled floors and glazed windows, free from animals except domestic pets. Some contemporaries, however, thought that these physical distinctions between noble and commoner denoted a racial difference – that nobles literally had purer blood and superior qualities of mind and body by descent. The sense that there was a separate noble caste was particularly acute after the Norman Conquest because Norman settlers had their own language: French became the language of their households in Britain, though its use was waning by the fourteenth century.

Despite this linguistic reinforcement of caste, nobility was not exclusive. It was possible (if exceptional) for the prosperous freeman or burgess to promote himself (or at least his descendants) into the nobility, either by the purchase of land held by feudal tenure, or by marriage to a noble heiress. By virtue of their offices and the benefices attached to them, the higher clergy also had noble status. A promising son of a peasant might have his school and university education paid for by a patron, who then employed him as a chaplain or administrator, and procured benefices to sustain and reward him. Some medieval bishops certainly had obscure origins.

The medieval noble, then, was distinguished by his appearance, his customary environment, and the superior quality of his clothing. Nobles also had distinctive manners, skills and life-styles. As squires they had a long apprenticeship in learning to fight on horseback and in the appropriate conventions of knightly conduct. Few among the lesser ranks of nobility, however, actually progressed to knighthood – the number of those dubbed substantially diminished in the thirteenth century – mainly because such promotion involved considerable expenditure (not least in the maintenance of warhorses). Yet these unknighted nobles continued to embrace knightly values, often commissioning armoured effigies for their tombs.

From the later twelfth century onwards, moreover, there was a growing stress in knightly education on the elements of chivalry appropriate to courtly life. The subject of the new style ballads and fictions was often the art of courtly love, which gave the lady a new role, where her aspirations, qualities and skills were valued as much as those of her noble lover. By feeding these new complexities into noble education, the landed nobility may have been unconsciously trying to distance itself from its inferiors, and to demonstrate its special lore and inherent superiority: at a time when the clergy were also developing a consciousness of superiority, and when new wealthy social groups were arising with their own special identity – the burgesses and merchants.

The secular nobility was only a tiny proportion of the total population, perhaps about one or two per cent, though they owned a large part of the land (their collective holdings being only rivalled by those of the king and the Church). Within the ranks of the nobility, however, there were extreme variations of wealth and corresponding distinctions in title and way of life. There was also considerable social mobility within these ranks – the ambition of poor squires and knights who lived by selling their swords was to be granted the marriage of an heiress by their lord: while at the lower end of the nobility there were always some who could not afford to maintain the appropriate standard of living, and consequently had to drop out by taking menial employment.

What was the role of the nobility in society? Under the prince, they were the rulers of the land, maintaining control over the peasantry through their stewards, bailiffs and reeves. As members of a feudal hierarchy, nobles in Britain also had traditional, well-understood, privileges and obligations. The wealthiest English and Scottish tenants-in-chief (the earls and barons) were the king's natural councillors, whose advice he ought to seek and heed in matters concerning the community of the realm: and they were expected to be among his principal military, diplomatic and governing agents. Knights who were the vassals of earls and barons fulfilled similar roles in the latter's lordships; gathering, when summoned, to give counsel in one of the lord's principal castles, just as the magnates themselves did at the king's court.

In Scotland widespread and sweeping powers of civil and criminal jurisdiction continued to be exercised in the private courts of regalities and baronies: and in parts of the Welsh principalities conquered by the Normans, (known as the Marches of Wales) lords continued to exercise princely powers of dispensing justice and levying dues. But in England, especially from the reign of Henry II (d.1189) onwards, the justice administered in the king's courts (by a corps of professional judges) came to overshadow the less comprehensive baronial justice. Henry and his successors also used the minor nobility as the agents of royal justice and administration in the shires. Thus vigorous royal administration not only induced the baronial tradition of protest, but also fostered the political consciousness of the minor nobility gathered together as shire communities. This political development was unique in medieval Britain, and was a significant factor in the development of a representative parliament.

The continued political and social eminence of the landed nobility was reflected in (and advertised by) their ostentatious way of life: and noble households were scaled-down versions of princely ones. An anonymous poem written in English after the mid fourteenth century in the Cheshire/Staffordshire borderlands, *Sir Gawain and the Green Knight*, gives a good picture of the ideals and aspirations of a provincial nobility. The castle of the Green Knight is literally and symbolically an oasis of civilisation amid the threatening wilderness. Its towers and battlements move the knightly traveller by their beauty, its residents place a high value on courtliness and good order, and its chambers are furnished luxuriously. The lord hunts with his male companions, while the lady presides over the household and entertains the noble guest. Yet the poet is not merely concerned with the surface gloss of noble life, but also with the spiritual qualities that should be at its core – the faith and loyalty which justified noble superiority.

CAERNARVON CASTLE
Gwynedd
OS 115 SH 477627

Caernarvon is on the north-west coast of Wales, eight miles south of Bangor on the A487: a few miles to the east is the spectacular landscape of the Snowdon mountain range, accessible via the A4086 along the edge of Llyn Padarn lake to Llanberis, and the Snowdon Mountain Railway from Llanberis to the summit.

The English medieval monarchy was an imperial one, with pretensions to overlordship or rule over the whole of the British Isles. It is, therefore in a way fitting that the power and majesty of English kingship can best be seen, not in England, but in the part of the British Isles which the English kings most successfully conquered – Wales. There it is displayed in the castles which Edward I built to subject and overawe the Welsh. Perhaps Caernarvon and Conwy castles give the best physical impression anywhere of English monarchy in its prime.

Caernarvon occupies an important strategic position: the Romans built a fort there (called Segontium), a few remains of which are in South Road. During the reign of William the Conqueror, Norman lords raided along the north Welsh coast. Hugh of Avranches, earl of Chester, built a motte and bailey castle here, on the peninsula formed by the Menai Strait, the river Seiont and the minor river Cadnant, which cuts across the base of the peninsula, but now flows underground. In 1283, when Edward I advanced to suppress the rebellion of Llywelyn Prince of Wales, work was begun to replace the Norman castle and to lay out a borough for English settlers, and a quay was constructed on the Menai Strait. In 1284, when Edward and his queen Eleanor were visiting Caernarvon, she gave birth to the future Edward II, probably in one of the timber-framed buildings erected in the half-finished castle. There was huge royal expenditure on the castle and town defences, which were mostly completed by 1288. In 1294 Llywelyn the Last's cousin Madoc ap Llywelyn revolted and seized Caernarvon, destroying much of the English works. In the next few years there was heavy expenditure on repairs, and the castle's defences on the town side were completed. The works at Caernarvon were practically completed by 1323.

The principal architect was James of St George (d.1308), who had worked for the counts of Savoy. The walls and multangular towers of the castle contrast with the lower walls (with round towers) of the surviving town defences. Outside these clustered the Welsh settlement; the natives were not allowed to live within the fortifications. The form of the castle towers and its decorative bands of contrasting stone bear a resemblance to the defences of Constantinople; this, it has been surmised, was intended to draw attention to Edward's imperial pretensions. The castle was the residence of the English justiciar of North Wales, the seat of government of the three shires which Edward established there.

The castle is divided into two wards: there are few traces of the courtyard buildings, but the towers, and curtain wall are well preserved. The main entrance, the King's Gate, faces the town at the junction between the lower and upper wards. A drawbridge led over the castle ditch to the gateway. To reach the lower ward through the King's Gate it would have been necessary to force five doors and six portcullises, making a right-hand turn and running a gauntlet of shot from arrow slits and from "murder holes" in the roof. At the end of the lower ward, facing the Menai Strait and the Seiont estuary, is the Eagle Tower (named after its heraldic decorations), a residence fit for a prince.

In the town, the fourteenth-century chapel of St Mary forms part of the town wall, and Eastgate Street is carried on a medieval bridge of six arches over the Cadnant. During the revolt of Owain Glyn Dŵr against Henry IV, Caernarvon was twice besieged unsuccessfully by the rebels, in 1403 and 1404. The castle fell into disrepair in the sixteenth century, but was held for Charles I in the Civil War. A careful restoration was carried out in the nineteenth century: in 1911 the future Edward VIII was invested as Prince of Wales in the castle, and Prince Charles was similarly honoured here in 1969.

The river-frontage of the castle, decorated with coloured stone banding.

The ruins of Caerphilly are some of the most impressive and extensive of any medieval castle, the most powerful expression remaining of the dominance of the aristocracy in medieval Britain. The castle was sited on low ground below Caerphilly Mountain, commanding the strategic route past it from the Severn valley. Building was commenced in about 1268 by Gilbert de Clare, Earl of Gloucester: the Clares were leading landowners in England, Wales and Ireland. Earl Gilbert's control and expansion of his Marcher lordship of Glamorgan was challenged by Prince Llywelyn: the building of the castle was an awesome response. Llywelyn vainly tried to stop the works by attack. The castle is a monument to the penultimate phase in the long struggle between the Welsh princes and Anglo-Normans, which Edward I resolved decisively in the next few decades by the conquest of all Wales.

The castle is, then, a brutal expression of empire-building and the imposition of colonial rule – by private enterprise, soon to be massively supplemented by state intervention. It was completed by the Despenser family in the early fourteenth century. Caerphilly Castle also represents (together with Edward I's Welsh castles) the acme of medieval military engineering and architecture. A lake was formed by damming two streams, forming two islands. On the larger of these are the main and earliest part of the defences

– two concentric rings of quadrangular curtain walls forming the inner and outer baileys. The dominating inner bailey has projecting circular angle towers and two opposed gateways protected by projecting pairs of horseshoe-shaped towers. The main domestic buildings lie along the south wall of the inner bailey and between its wall and that of the outer bailey. The great hall, dating from the early fourteenth century, has fine sculptured features. The western gatehouse of the outer ward, in front of that of the inner ward, was connected via a drawbridge to the island, which was walled. This island was perhaps intended as a refuge for peasants and cattle.

The eastern gatehouse of the outer bailey, similarly positioned, was connected by a drawbridge at the narrowest point of the lake to the most remarkable feature of the castle's defences – a barrage-like barbican, a series of moated stone screens with outward-projecting towers and sluice gates, built across almost the full width of the lake.

The castle certainly fulfilled the purpose of holding the Welsh in check. In 1294–95 and 1316 rebels failed to capture it, though on the former occasion they burnt many houses in the borough nearby. In the divisions of the Clare inheritance after the death of Earl Gilbert at Bannockburn in 1314, Caerphilly was part of the lion's share received by Edward II's favourite Hugh Despenser the Younger, who was to pay for his presumption

CAERPHILLY CASTLE
Mid Glamorgan
OS 171 ST 157871

The castle stands in the middle of Caerphilly, which is seven miles north of Cardiff city centre via the A469: its setting is the grimly beautiful industrial landscape of the Welsh Valleys.

The complex fortifications at Caerphilly actually pre-date by nearly ten years those at Flint, the earliest of Edward I's ring of castles in north Wales.

27

with his life. In 1326 Roger Mortimer of Wigmore, who had opposed him, and Queen Isabella (Roger's lover) invaded England. Edward II soon found support crumbling and fled to South Wales, where he stayed at Caerphilly Castle trying to raise forces. Soon after leaving he was captured, but the castle had to be besieged before his captain there, Sir John Felton, surrendered it. In 1337 the Despensers got their forfeited castle back and held it until Thomas Despenser forfeited it in 1400 for trying to put another unfortunate king, Richard II, back on the throne.

During the fifteenth century Caerphilly was held by members of leading magnate families, the Beauchamps and Nevilles, including Warwick "the Kingmaker". Through his heirs it came to the Crown and was granted in 1550 by Edward VI to Sir William Herbert, who allowed it to decay. It was not besieged in the Civil War, but eventually rendered indefensible. A curious memento of this 'dismantling' is the south-east tower of the inner bailey, the outer half of which leans ten degrees from the vertical – the result of an attempt to demolish it with explosives. A lengthy and careful modern restoration of the castle has been undertaken, begun by the Marquess of Bute in the nineteenth century. *See* **Beaumaris, Harlech**

CAMBUSKENNETH ABBEY
Central
OS 57 NS 808939
The abbey stands by the River Forth about a mile east of Stirling, from which it is accessible via the A9 north, the A91 towards Alloa, and then a signposted minor road. Nearby Stirling Castle is also well worth a visit, as is the Bannockburn battle site and museum to the south-east of the town.

Cambuskenneth Abbey was a house of Augustinian canons founded by David I in 1147. It received many endowments from Scottish kings and nobles – who often visited it since it was near the royal castle of Stirling – and became one of the richer Scottish monasteries. Edward I stayed there in 1303–4; there Scottish barons met in 1308 to swear to be faithful to his opponent Robert Bruce. In 1326, near the end of Bruce's reign, leading Scots magnates gathered there to swear fealty to his little son and heir, the future David II.

Little of any height remains of the abbey church. But the thirteenth century bell-tower remains intact, a solid, restrained composition with lancet windows and decorative arcading. This tower, unusual in being detached, seems unnecessary, a luxury – except that it advertised the wealth of the house and the importance which the canons attached to the celebration of religious services.

In 1864, a tomb slab of blue stone and two skeletons were discovered before the High Altar, thought to be the burial of James III (d.1488) and his queen, Margaret of Denmark. They were re-interred beneath a new inscription. It was because of her father's inability to pay her dower in full that James had retained Orkney and Shetland in pledge – never to be redeemed from the Scottish Crown, despite the efforts of later Danish kings. King James was killed at nearby Sauchieburn, after a battle with rebels led by his own son. He had gone hopefully into battle, carrying Robert the Bruce's sword, near the site of the Bruce's great victory of Bannockburn: but almost at once he fell from his horse and was carried unconscious to a mill, where he was squalidly murdered by a man disguised as a priest. His and Margaret's portraits, by the Flemish artist Hugo van der Goes, can be seen in the wonderful Trinity College Altarpiece, now in in the National Gallery at Edinburgh.

CANTERBURY Kent
OS 179 TR 152578
Canterbury, one of the most interesting and beautiful cities in England, is some sixty miles south east of London by the A2 and M2 motorways, and is a convenient stopping place on the way to Dover and Europe. Comparatively small, and easily explored on foot, Canterbury is packed with architectural treasures: notably the cathedral and its precinct, the towering medieval walls, and many ancient timber-framed houses in the streets around the cathedral, especially Palace Street, Burghgate and Northgate.

Canterbury's origins as a city stem from a flourishing Roman settlement, and it was also important in the Jutish kingdom of Kent: there in 597 King Ethelbert of Kent permitted St Augustine and his fellow monks, (reluctant missionaries sent from Rome into a distant pagan land by Pope Gregory the Great) to perform Christian worship in public and to start a mission. The monastery founded by St Augustine, (later known as St Augustine's Abbey) flourished in the Middle Ages. The extensive ruins of its successive early churches can be seen outside the city wall, off Broad Street, where stands the imposing monastic great gatehouse (1300–9).

Nothing is visible, however, of the Anglo-Saxon cathedral. For during the archiepiscopate of Lanfranc, William the Conqueror's respected councillor, a larger building was begun, and Lanfranc's successor St Anselm supervised the building of the choir and eastern transepts. Only the shell of these eastern parts remains, as they were gutted by fire in 1174, while Lanfranc's nave and transepts were replaced in the fourteenth century; work commenced on a new nave in 1378 and continued for almost a century. The great west window has fifteenth century glass. The central tower, nicknamed Bell Harry Tower, dates from c.1490; the one prominent remaining feature of Lanfranc's church, the north-west tower, was replaced in the early nineteenth century by a replica of the early fifteenth century south-west tower. The crypt has Norman pillars and arches with a wealth of carved capitals.

In 1170 one of the most famous events in medieval history occurred in the cathedral – the murder by Henry II's enraged knights of Archbishop Thomas Becket, at the spot in the north-west transept known as the Martyrdom. The cult of the martyr quickly spread through Western Europe, and Canterbury became a major place of pilgrimage. In 1538, however, Henry VIII's commissioners had the shrine demolished and cartloads of jewels and other

The tomb and funeral achievements of Edward, The Black Prince.

precious offerings taken away from it; but even then St Thomas's name was so potent that Henry had him denounced by proclamation as a traitor.

The development of the cult gave the monks an incentive to rebuild the burnt part of the cathedral on a magnificent scale. The work was supervised by a French mason, William of Sens, who introduced the new "Gothic" style of the Ile de France – tall piers with delicate clusters of marble shafts, naturalistically carved capitals, pointed arches and ribbed vaults. Then, while standing on scaffolding to supervise work over the vault over the High Altar, "French William" was disabled by a fall. His task was taken over by William "the Englishman", who continued the work eastwards, building the Trinity Chapel to house the shrine of St Thomas and the semi-circular Corona or Crown to house the severed crown of the martyr's head. The eastern rebuilding was completed by 1184.

The stone screens round the choir date from 1285–1331. Among the medieval prelates buried there is Archbishop Simon Sudbury, beheaded by rebels in London on Tower Hill during the Peasants' Revolt of 1381. Off the south choir aisle is St Anselm's chapel with a fine early fresco of St Paul and a five-light Decorated window of 1336. The Trinity Chapel, to the east of the presbytery, is on the site of the chapel where St Thomas said his first Mass as archbishop, and in whose crypt he was at first buried. On the south side of the Trinity Chapel (near the place where the martyr's shrine was ultimately raised) is the tomb and military effigy of Edward III's son Edward Prince of Wales (d.1376), known to posterity as the Black Prince. He had a high reputation as a chivalrous knight and skilled commander – he was the victor of the battles of Poitiers (1356) and Najera in Castile (1367). Under the wooden canopy over the tomb is a rare example of English panel painting from the period, a depiction of the Trinity, to which the prince had a particular devotion. Round the canopy and on the pillars are the hooks on which hung black tapestry bordered with crimson – giving the tomb some resemblance to the great beds which were among the most luxurious furnishings of contemporary aristocratic houses. Miraculously, some of the prince's funeral accoutrements survived, suspended on a cross beam above the canopy – his helmet, heraldic tabard, brazen gauntlets and wooden shield: these would have been carried in his funeral procession (the originals are now displayed under glass, and have been replaced by replicas). On the north side of the Trinity Chapel, opposite the Black Prince's tomb, is the monument of Henry IV (d.1413) and his queen Joan of Navarre – Henry was responsible for the deposition and death of the Black Prince's son Richard II. The royal couple's effigies appear to be attempts at portraiture, contrasting with the prince's conventional knightly appearance.

One of the cathedral's great treasures is its collection of stained glass windows in the eastern parts, unrivalled for their period (late twelfth and early thirteenth centuries) anywhere else in England. There are illustrations of Biblical themes concentrating on the significance of Christ, and of saints' lives: and in the Trinity Chapel miracles performed by St Thomas are depicted. For instance, in one of the windows of the north aisle is the miracle of Rodbertulus ("Bobby") of Rochester, an eight-year-old who was drowned in the Medway whilst throwing stones at frogs. His playmates told his parents, who fished his body out at low tide, and through their prayers to St Thomas the boy recovered. Then there is Matilda of Cologne, a maniac who murdered her baby. Her keepers beat her with cudgels as she went on pilgrimage

to St Thomas, and as she collapsed from the blows at the tomb she regained her sanity. She gives thanks while a monk places a candle on the tomb; the keepers stand by, cudgels at rest.

Considerable remains of the buildings of the cathedral priory survive, including the partly Norman chapter-house, the mainly fourteenth century cloisters and Christ Church Gateway (1517). An unusual building is the twelfth century water tower, whose cistern provided water piped to the living quarters of prior and monks.

Canterbury probably had resident traders in the ninth century and in 1086 it was among the larger English towns, with a gild merchant. It flourished in the Middle Ages, providing services for the city's religious houses and pilgrims; and for long it produced high quality cloth. The city, near the south coast, was more vulnerable to invasion than most in England; stretches of its well-maintained walls survive, and remains of the twelfth century keep of the royal castle. The castle fell into decay in the Middle Ages, but when (in the late 1370s) Kent was threatened by French and Castilian raids, the formidable Westgate was built to strengthen the defences of the city wall – an early example of a fortification designed for defence by cannon.

The continued vulnerability of the city was again apparent during the 1939–45 War when much of its medieval centre was destroyed by bombing. Yet a number of fragments of medieval buildings remain, such as the Hospital of St Thomas the Martyr (later Eastbridge Hospital), a resting-place for pilgrims; the Greyfriars (the earliest Franciscan house in England, founded in 1224); the Poor Priests' Hospital, also in Stour Street; and the Dominican house in Blackfriars.

Norman arcading progressively submerged by the medieval staircase in the north aisle.

In 1092 William Rufus took Carlisle, erected a castle there on the high ground above the river Eden and brought in English peasant colonists to strengthen his hold on a region strongly independent in character. Henry I appointed a bishop here in 1133, and Augustinian canons were endowed to serve the cathedral. In the twelfth and thirteenth centuries the Scottish Crown disputed control of Cumbria – Stephen ceded it to David I, who died in Carlisle Castle in 1153: but in 1237 Alexander II finally relinquished the Scottish claim and recognised a frontier between England and Scotland approximating to the present one. The castle was an important base for Edward I's attempts to subdue the Scots. The town and region were to reap the whirlwind: Carlisle remained a frontier post with a royal garrison for about three hundred years: and the town gates only ceased to be manned and closed at night in 1625, so insecure were local conditions even after the Union of the Crowns in 1603.

During the later Middle Ages, moreover, Carlisle had to endure several sieges. After Robert I's victory at Bannockburn in 1314 the Scots strenuously invested Carlisle, assaulting the castle with siege catapults, a "belfry" and mining. But a local knight, Andrew de Harcla, kept them out. The Scots besieged Carlisle again in 1379 and 1385; and Lancastrian diehards attacked it in 1461. The Union of the Crowns did not end its role in Anglo-Scottish warfare. The Scots besieged and captured it in 1644 on behalf of the English Parliament. The royalists briefly held it again in 1648. In 1745 a scratch force all too briefly held the castle against the Jacobite Highland Army. After the capitulation Prince Charles Edward Stuart ("Bonny Prince Charlie") came in from Brampton and proclaimed his father king at Carlisle Cross. On his retreat from England he left a garrison in the castle, which soon had to surrender to George II's son the Duke of Cumberland.

Locked into an insecure frontier, and lacking good communications even with Newcastle, Carlisle remained a small market town and port, catering for the needs of the canons, the local gentry and the castle garrison. It had royal charters of privileges, a mayor and corporation, and a gild merchant: but it could boast only two parishes and two friaries. Experience taught the locals that they could not always rely on a usually distraught king to provide them with an effective defence against the Scots. As Professor Barrie Dobson has pointed out, the townsmen regarded themselves as under the special protection of the Virgin Mary, whose status in their cathedral they revered. When the Scots besieged the city in 1385, it was the Virgin who came to the rescue by her appearance, striking terror into the Scots with her warning and display of the royal banner. She "often appeared to the inhabitants of that city" commented an English chronicler.

Only a fragment of the medieval cathedral remains, albeit an impressive one. There are two full bays of the twelfth century Romanesque church – the rest were pulled down by the Scots after they had captured the castle in 1644, in order to strengthen the defences. The south transept has Romanesque features: the north transept was rebuilt probably in the early fifteenth century. The sturdy central tower also dates from this period. The large, wide choir is well preserved; part of it dates from c.1220–50, part is a rebuilding of the early fourteenth century, probably consequent on the fire of 1292. The east window with its elaborate tracery fills up the east end. As Professor R. L. Storey has remarked, this rebuilding of the east end at a time of great menace from the Scots was a notable act of faith by the canons. Here, in this remote, insecure, poor region, they had this glorious design created. Perhaps they and the townsmen already shared a conviction that the Virgin would give protection.

The cathedral has some of its medieval furnishings, notably the canopied early fifteenth century choir stalls. On the backs of the stalls, facing the aisles, are a series of paintings illustrating saints' lives, including scenes from the life of St Cuthbert, dear to the hearts of many borderers. There are remains of some of the conventual buildings within the cathedral close (which had a medieval precinct wall) – the undercroft of the dormitory, the refectory and the gatehouse. The Prior's Tower, battlemented and of three stages, is a defensible residence, though it stood within the city walls (of which fragments remain). The prior's room on the first floor was fitted out by Simon Senhouse (prior 1500–1520) with oriel windows, the fireplace, and the marvellously preserved and gaily coloured paintings on the ceilings in forty-five panels. Here one gets a better impression of the living room of a Border noble of the period than anywhere else. The prior's bedroom, on the second floor, is now a museum.

Carlisle Castle is worth visiting, though sieges and continued military usage have obliterated or obscured medieval features. In particular the character of the outer bailey has been changed by the raising of its level in the nineteenth century to form a barrack square. But the curtain walls of the outer and inner baileys remain, and so do their respective gatehouses. The most impressive feature is the twelfth century keep standing within the inner bailey.

See **Bothwell**

CARLISLE Cumbria
OS 85 NY 397563
Carlisle stands near the Anglo-Scottish frontier 300 miles north-east of London by the M1 and M6 and some 150 miles south-east of Edinburgh via the picturesque A7 route through the Border hills. The cathedral is near the station, and the castle somewhat to the north of the city centre. Carlisle is an excellent centre for exploring the Borders and nearby Hadrian's Wall.

Life in the Medieval Town

Market and fair days were times when characteristic urban activities were at their height, when the character of towns was temporarily transformed, and when their relations with their environment became most intense. Some small places must have been regularly turned into a caravanserai by the influx of fair-time incomers – sometimes expressly termed "foreigners" in civic records. Village-sized towns engaged mainly in agricultural production tended to be well integrated with rural society, but there were often tensions between the inhabitants of large towns and "foreigners". Craft gildsmen were suspicious that the latter sold substandard goods and undercut the locals. Townsmen sneered at countryfolk as bumpkins; while countrymen complained of being cozened and cheated by city hucksters, petty thieves and prostitutes. In some cities, indeed, "foreign" merchants were compelled to lodge with a native trader, who could keep an eye on their transactions.

Urban governments laid down the conditions under which burgesses and strangers could trade, and special courts of "piepowder" (the "dusty feet" of travellers) were set up by them to regulate market disputes. Town elites were also much concerned about the problem of disorder, and not only when towns were swelled by a motley throng of strangers: for life in larger towns was particularly conducive to violence. Folk often lived in crowded conditions on the margins of subsistence; men carried knives and were quick to draw them; prostitution was rife, and prostitutes outraged decency by imitating the fine clothes of the nobility in order to advertise themselves.

Civic authorities likewise tried to control the population by having a curfew imposed at nightfall, for anyone abroad in the dark was assumed to be up to no good in medieval society. Town gates were shut; watchmen scanned the darkness and patrolled the streets. But there were problems for some authorities in enforcing order, especially when suburbs developed which were sometimes outside their jurisdiction, whither fugitives fled from arrest, and where uncontrolled craftsmen plied their trades. Just outside London, for instance, was Southwark, on the far side of the Thames and beyond the city's power, notorious for its thieves and brothels. Some cities also had the problem of a "liberty", an independent enclave held by a lord or ecclesiastical institution actually within their walls: this was a constant source of friction since its inhabitants were not subject to civic regulation, it acted as a sanctuary for fugitives, and its officers tended to be uncooperative.

But there was a more fundamental reason why authorities in larger towns found it difficult to maintain an orderly society: for that society was to a large extent an immigrant one. Many urban families originated in the countryside and were uprooted both from their communities and from the conventions which had traditionally regulated their behaviour. Loyalties and standards therefore had to be manufactured anew, and the roles of the urban parish and the craft gild were important in achieving this. The parish defined the people living in a small area as sharing a set of obligations to its priest and church, punishable by ecclesiastical courts if not fulfilled: and these courts might also impose penances for unsocial behaviour. Some of the shared obligations necessitated group activity, religious and financial, and a focus for group loyalty was provided by the parochial saint, whose banner and perhaps whose relic would be carried in processions. Production in a particular craft also tended to be concentrated in one parish. Craft gilds regulated conditions of production and employment and defined the status of their members by imposing a hierarchy. Such craft gilds often had their chapels in the parish church, where gildsmen (under penalty of fine) attended Mass on the gild holiday or to commemorate deceased brothers. Gild members were thus tied together not just as competitors and as masters and servants, but as brethren with shared spiritual obligations.

The loyalties created in big towns were therefore essentially local: there was an adaptation of the customs of the rural parish to changed conditions. The rise of public spectacle – processions, tableaux, plays – in larger towns was stimulated by the need to demonstrate the connection of these parochial loyalties to a larger whole. On civic holidays there were processions of mayor and corporation in which the craft gilds participated, defining their place in the community by an order of precedence. Civic spectacle was educational, didactic, exciting and entertaining. A king who made a "state entry" into a city might be greeted by mayor, aldermen and gilds in their robes, by processions of sacred relics from the parish churches and religious houses and by tableaux of angels and prophets. Such images and ceremonies projected an ideal of the city's relationship with the realm and with the divinely ordained universe. Perhaps they gave meaning even to the lives of the urban poor.

CARREG CENNEN CASTLE
Dyfed
OS 159 SN 666188

The castle towers over the River Cennen near Trapp village, some two and a half miles south-east of Llandeilo (which has its own fine castle of Dynevor): to the north, between Llandeilo and Lampeter, is the wild and almost uninhabited landscape of the Cambrian Mountains.

There was an ancient Welsh stronghold on this spectacular site – a limestone crag with precipitous sides, separated from a range of hills by the river Cennen, and rising nearly 300 feet above the river valley. It was part of the lordship of Dynevor, and was captured by the English only in 1277, when Payn de Chaworth seized it during Edward I's invasion of Wales. In 1282 the castle fell to Prince Llywelyn's brother Dafydd, when they revolted against Edward. The Earl of Gloucester led an expedition which recovered it, and a scratch English garrison of fifty managed to hold out there. Next year Edward granted the castle and surrounding lordship to a veteran soldier, John Giffard of Brimpsfield (Gloucestershire). His son was hanged at Gloucester in 1322 for supporting the rebellion of Thomas of Lancaster against Edward II. In 1340 the castle came into the hands of Thomas's brother Earl Henry; from then on it was a Lancastrian (and from 1399 royal) fortress. In 1403 it was taken by Owain Glyn Dŵr: and in 1462 the partisans of Edward IV captured it from the supporters of Henry VI and then broke down its defences to stop it being occupied as a stronghold against the new Yorkist regime. Henry VII granted the castle to his leading supporter in Wales, Rhys ap Thomas.

There are considerable remains of the defences built, it has been surmised, by the Giffards. The nucleus of the castle is a rectangular ward whose main defences are concentrated on the less precipitous northern side, including a strong gatehouse with projecting multangular towers. Along the eastern wall is the principal domestic range, with kitchen, hall, chapel and solar. To the north and east the inner bailey is surrounded by an outer one with curtain wall and three semicircular angle towers. But the most elaborate defence work is the long barbican in the outer bailey, set mainly at right angles to the gatehouse of the inner bailey, which forced the attacker into a narrow passageway studded with pits, doors and drawbridges. Advance through this barbican required two rightangle turns, and was exposed to fire from the inner bailey's battlements. The castle also has a unique feature – an underground passage hewn through rock, leading to a cave under the outer bailey, which perhaps provided a specially secure and secret storage-space. The cave, however, was certainly in existence before the castle, and prehistoric remains have been found there.

CHEPSTOW CASTLE Gwent
OS 174 ST 534942

Chepstow is at the northern end of the Severn Bridge, which carries the M4 from Bristol across the Severn Estuary into South Wales. Respectively five and fifteen miles to the north are Tintern Abbey and historic Monmouth, both reached from Chepstow via the beautiful A466 road through the wooded Wye Valley: and to the north-east is the Forest of Dean.

The town of Chepstow was sited in a strong defensive position formed by a loop in the river Wye, to guard against Welsh incursions. The castle has an elongated plan, its three baileys and barbican following the configuration of a narrow spur of land on high ground above the river, bounded to the south by a ravine. The rectangular keep in the inner bailey was built in William the Conqueror's time by William Fitz Osbern, as part of a fortress to control the lands which he had seized from the Welsh. His descendant Isabel de Clare brought Chepstow by marriage to the Marshal family, and they held it till 1245. Subsequently it was in the hands of other magnate families – the earls and dukes of Norfolk, the Welsh Herberts under Edward IV, and the Somersets during and after the rule of their Tudor kinsmen. In 1645 the castle's walls were breached by Parliamentarian artillery, but it was repaired and garrisoned till 1690, after which it was allowed to decay.

The castle was extensively remodelled and extended in the thirteenth century, and despite later destruction and alteration, much of this work survives. In this period the keep was remodelled and, to the east, a lower bailey was built beyond what is now the middle bailey. The lower bailey's great gatehouse has semi-circular towers: and the bailey's defences are dominated by Marten's Tower, which commands the approaches to the great gatehouse and the south-eastern curtain wall. Notice the thickened 'spur walls' (a precaution against undermining) at the base of this tower, which is named after Henry Marten, a signatory of Charles I's death warrant imprisoned there after the restoration of Charles II. The lower bailey has an impressive range of thirteenth century domestic buildings: the barbican at the west end of the castle dates from the same period, as do the remnants of the town walls, and the Town Gate across the High Street.

Much of the ruined structure of Chepstow Castle to be seen today, dates from the thirteenth century.

CHIPCHASE CASTLE
Northumberland
OS 87 NY 918735

The castle is some twenty-seven miles north-west of Newcastle-upon-Tyne, via the A69 to Corbridge, the A68 towards Jedburgh (the Roman Dere Street), the A6079 west, and a minor road through Barrasford. A mile or so to the south is a fine stretch of Hadrian's Wall, with the remains of several Roman forts.

Chipchase castle is a good early example of a Border pele-tower. It stands on the bank of the river North Tyne, with a gentle slope from it to the river; and this handsome rectangular building was intended to offer serious resistance to Scottish raids. The walls, nine feet thick at the base and faced with fine ashlar, rise fifty feet to a parapet walk, corbelled and machicolated. Four watch turrets rise and project from the top, also machicolated. There are four floors: entrance is to the ground floor (a vaulted basement) by means of a door which still has its portcullis. A circular staircase leads to the other floors, and the chambers from which the portcullis was worked is on the first floor. The living quarters were on the second and third floors: on the third there is a well-lit hall and a kitchen.

The property belonged in the thirteenth and early fourteenth centuries to the Lisle family. In 1348 Sir Robert de Lisle sold the marriage of his granddaughter Cecile, the heiress of Chipchase, to a leading Northumberland knight, William Heron of Ford, on condition that Heron married Cecile to one of his sons. It is tempting to connect the building of this impressive pele-tower with the acquisition of Chipchase by the Herons. Attached to the tower is a much larger mansion built by Cuthbert Heron in about 1621, when times had become more peaceful.

CLAVERLEY Shropshire
OS 138 SO 792934

Claverley is five miles east of Bridgnorth, via the A454 towards Wolverhampton and a minor road turning south in Wyken.

The church of All Saints was founded by Roger de Montgomery (d.1094), one of William the Conqueror's Norman followers. The king granted him Claverley and other estates in Shropshire. The nave arcades of the church date from the twelfth and thirteenth centuries and were part of a rebuilding of an earlier church on a bigger scale, while the impressive chancel is a rebuilding of the mid-fourteenth century. The porch and upper part of the tower are among the fifteenth century additions.

Above the chancel arch are the remains of a medieval painting of the Last Judgement – a subject often painted there to warn and edify congregations. There are also outstandingly interesting wall paintings on the north side of the nave, notably a frieze above the arcade dating from c.1200. This shows fifteen knights on horseback, five pairs of them fighting with lances and spears. The subject-matter has been identified as a (now incomplete) illustration of an early Christian poem, the *Psychomachia* by Prudentius (d.410), which describes combats between seven Christian virtues and seven pagan vices. In this painting we also see represented the sort of knight who went on crusade with Richard I and who skirmished locally in the Marches of Wales. The painting shows how, as a result of the "Twelfth Century Renaissance", peasants living in a remote frontier region had an opportunity to acquire ideas derived from a sub-classical Latin poem.

COBHAM Kent
OS 178 TQ 670684

The picturesque village of Cobham is some thirty miles south-east of London and four miles west of Rochester, and is signposted south via a minor road off the A2 trunk road, shortly before this merges with the M2. The church stands opposite the famous Leather Bottle Inn, and the delightful college quadrangle (which is open to the public) is immediately south of the church.

Cobham parish church is a good example of one rebuilt on an imposing scale in the thirteenth and fourteenth centuries. The chancel is a reconstruction of the early thirteenth century, with fine lancet windows: but the nave and its aisles were rebuilt and the tower added by the patron of the benefice, John Lord Cobham (d.1408). This rebuilding, the tombs of Cobham and other lords of the manor in the church, and the alteration in its usage affected by him illustrate the impact which a noble could have on parochial life. In 1362 Cobham founded a chantry, with an endowment for a master and four other priests. They were to say Masses in the church choir for the souls whom Cobham wished to have commemorated. From 1370 onwards their college dwelling was erected south of the church, where they were to live under corporate rules. A quadrangle of this survives, with the priests' dining hall; it was converted into almshouses after the Reformation, and is still used as such.

Cobham was one of a number of knights who fought successfully in Edward III's brutally conducted wars in France and who were conspicuous by their religious benefactions. On his memorial brass in the church he had himself depicted in plate armour. The knight who has fought faithfully in his lord's wars, but not in Christ's has something to offer for his soul's welfare: for he is shown holding an elegant model of the church he has beautified. In old age, in 1398, Cobham had the humiliating experience of being convicted of treason – Richard II had long harboured a political grudge against him. But he allowed the old man to go into exile on the island of Jersey, whence he was soon to be recalled for reinstatement by Henry IV.

There are altogether seventeen fine monumental brasses in the church, forming the finest collection in Britain: all but one of them are pre-sixteenth century, and nearly all commemorate members of the Cobham family. Cobham Hall, the core of which dates from the late Elizabethan period, is one of the major country houses of Kent.

In the seventh century Coldingham was within the Anglo-Saxon kingdom of Northumbria. King Oswy's sister Ebba came there in 640 to join the community of nuns and monks, over which she was to preside as abbess – she is still commemorated in the name of St Abb's Head, the nearby rocky promontory jutting dramatically into the North Sea. The monastic community was broken up by the Danish attack in 870: and in 1098 Edgar king of Scots gave the property to Durham Priory, which in the twelfth century developed a cell there staffed by its monks. Well endowed, Coldingham Priory ruled the fertile Berwickshire region of Coldinghamshire and was able to sustain thirty monks at the end of the thirteenth century. But the Scottish Wars of Independence were soon to leave the priory vulnerably placed near the embattled Anglo-Scottish frontier. Scots became suspicious of these English monks within their borders, and covetous of their wealth, though depleted. In 1378 Robert II granted the priory to Dunfermline Abbey (Fife). Next year the Coldingham monks were accused by Scottish ecclesiastics of large-scale espionage, sending Scottish bullion to England, smuggling the bones of St Margaret and St Ebba there and terrorising the neighbourhood with hired soldiers.

Durham recovered control of Coldingham by the 1390s, but the last English monks were expelled by 1462. Long before then a rising local family had extended its interested pro-

tection over the priory – the Humes (from whom the former Prime Minister, Lord Hume of the Hirsel, is descended). In the 1470s and 1480s James III tried to annex the priory revenues to royal religious foundations. This provoked the Humes and led to the revolt in which James died at Sauchieburn in 1488. In the sixteenth century the priors were mostly laymen, Humes and Stewarts, and the number of monks dwindled away. The priory was besieged by the invading English in 1537, 1547 and 1648, and Cromwell tried to blow it up.

It is surprising, therefore, that there is anything left to be seen of the priory in Coldingham village, in its isolated rural setting just inland from the wild coast. Indeed, there are only fragments of the monastic buildings above ground. But the chancel of the priory church was restored as the parish church in 1662. The exterior is austere, much of it being post-medieval, but inside is a revelation. There is a double tier of arcades on the north and east walls dating from the thirteenth century. The upper tier is best preserved, and this alternates lancet windows with free-standing arcades, with a variety of fine naturalistic carvings on the capitals. It is a pleasing rhythmic composition, delicately executed – a fruit, probably, of the Durham connection. Here one is in the civilised world of international Gothic culture, soon to be threatened by the barbarisms of prolonged frontier warfare.

COLDINGHAM PRIORY
Borders
OS 67 NT 904659
Coldingham village is some fifty-five miles east of Edinburgh and three miles north-west of Eyemouth, on the A1107 from Eyemouth to Dunbar. The nearby coastline is craggy and dramatic.

Occupying a commanding position overlooking the Don valley, Conisbrough Castle is enclosed by the mighty earthworks of an earlier Norman fortress. Its most striking feature, however, is the splendid keep raised in about 1190 by Henry II's bastard half-brother Hamelin Plantagenet, and so well preserved that its recently-cleaned stonework gleams almost like new. Surrounded by slightly later curtain walls with solid round towers, this remarkable keep is a cylinder nearly ninety feet high, clasped by six great wedge-shaped buttresses which rise to roof-top height and serve as turrets: unique in England (though Hamelin built a similar keep in Normandy)

its design was intended to obviate the structural right-angles so notoriously vulnerable to undermining or bombardment by siege engines. Though it is now roofless and floorless, the keep's interior architecture is also in excellent condition, testifying to the high quality of Hamelin's masons. It contained four circular storeys, the third being the great hall – with a stone wash-basin and a lavatory in the thickness of the wall – and the storey above the lord's private room, with a tiny but still beautiful chapel hollowed into one of the buttresses: both these chambers also have fine fireplaces, with cunningly constructed lintels of "joggled" mortarless masonry.

CONISBROUGH CASTLE
South Yorkshire
OS 111 SK 515989
Set amid heavily industrialised landscape north-east of Conisbrough town centre, the castle towers above the A630, four and a half miles south-west of Doncaster and about two miles west of the main A1(M) trunk road, from which it is easily accessible: it is open all year. The nearby parish church contains a remarkable Norman tomb chest, carved with fighting knights and fantastic beasts.

There are similarities between the foundations of castles and boroughs at Conwy and Caernarvon by Edward I during his 1283 campaigns – and indeed with his other colonial foundations in Wales. The site at Conwy did not have such good natural water defences as that at Caernarvon: it lay between the broad estuary of the river Conwy and the minor Gyffin stream flowing into it. But Conwy Castle, built at the point of confluence, has the additional strength of standing on a steep rocky outcrop. The relationship of its defences to those of the

new English borough was similar to that at Caernarvon, and both places had the same architect – James of St George.

The works at Conwy were completed by 1287: there were few subsequent additions. The towers and remaining domestic buildings are all roofless. Eight towers loom up over the estuary, studding the curtain wall which surrounds an inner and an outer ward. The approach to the outer ward from the town was via a ramp, then by a drawbridge across the moat. The intruder who had got this far would find himself corralled in a barbican,

CONWY CASTLE Gwynedd
OS 115 SH 785775
The castle and walled town of Conwy stand on the north coast of Wales, at the point where the main A55 crosses the Conwy estuary on its way to Holyhead and the Irish Sea ferry. A short trip south down the A470 takes the traveller into mountainous Snowdonia, and within reach to the west are Conwy's sister castles of Beaumaris and Caernarvon.

The intricacies of the castle layout seen from the east end of the wall walk, with the Bakehouse Tower in the foreground on the left. Right, an expression of freedom within the Prison Tower.

pelted with shot from the two great western towers. From the barbican a gateway between them led to the outer ward, in which there are remains of the great hall. Access from the outer to the inner ward was through a gate protected by a drawbridge over a pit adjacent to the well. The inner ward perhaps gives the best surviving impression anywhere of a royal residence used by an English king on his travels. Its four towers are turreted, and designed to fly standards. The two western towers were for service rooms, the two eastern ones formed part of the royal residence, together with the first floors of the courtyard buildings – a dining hall, a reception room (the "presence chamber") and a private suite. Beyond the eastern towers there is a barbican similar to that adjoining the outer ward at the other end of the castle, but larger, and with stairs down to a watergate

The southern profile of the castle bordered by the Gyffin Stream and, above, a view of its turreted towers.

for embarkation on the Conwy estuary.

In 1294 Edward I probably stayed in these apartments during Madoc ap Llywelyns' revolt. So probably did Richard II when he arrived here in 1399 from South Wales, to realise that his rebellious cousin Henry of Lancaster controlled Cheshire, and that his military position was hopeless. But Richard bravely – or foolhardily – rejected the option of sailing to France from the Conwy estuary, and eventually fell into Henry's hands at *Flint*. In 1401, at an early stage of Owain Glyn Dŵr's revolt against Henry's rule, Owain's kinsmen Gwilym and Rhys ap Tudur ap Gronw of Penmynydd in Anglesey seized the castle: but they surrendered to the constable of the castle, "Hotspur". Conwy decayed in the sixteenth century, but it was garrisoned for Charles I in the Civil War and, after its surrender in 1646, for Parliament. An order was made for it to be rendered indefensible in 1655.

Edward's I's town walls survive: so does the English settlers' parish church. This had been built in the twelfth century as part of a Cistercian monastery whose Welsh monks Edward removed. It was the burial place of a notable Prince of Wales, Llywelyn ap Iorwerth (d.1240). There are some fine old buildings in the town, for instance the later medieval Aberconway, at the junction of High Street and Castle Street, and Plas Mawr (1576), at the corner of Crown Lane and High Street. The challenge of bridging the estuary produced outstanding Victorian engineering feats, namely Thomas Telford's suspension bridge (1826) and Robert Stephenson's even more remarkable tubular railway bridge (1848) alongside it.

See **Caernarvon, Flint, Trotton**

The Stockhouse Tower overlooks the castle's outer ward to the west.

CORBRIDGE Northumberland
OS 87 NY 988644

The attractive town of Corbridge is sixteen miles west of Newcastle-upon-Tyne via the A69: the vicar's pele stands in the churchyard of the impressive Anglo-Saxon and thirteenth century church, near the Tyne Bridge. One and a half miles north of Corbridge is Aydon Castle, and three miles to the west is Hexham Abbey.

In the twelfth and thirteenth centuries Corbridge was a prosperous royal borough, but it suffered as a result of the Scottish Wars of Independence and their aftermath of Anglo-Scottish hostility. It was dangerously exposed to raids by invasion forces and was sacked by the Scots in 1296, 1311 and 1346. Yet it continued to exist as a market centre: and the adaptation of the inhabitants to less secure frontier conditions is reflected by the building in the early fourteenth century of the

pele-tower on one side of the Market Place, next to the church. This was said in 1415 to be the "vicar's pele". So presumably it was paid for by Carlisle Priory (which held the rectory), and the canons anticipated that there would continue to be worthwhile parochial revenues and a succession of resident parish priests. Like other northern English clergy, the Corbridge parish priest, despite the prohibition of canon law, would be expected to possess arms and wield them in emergencies;

the pele-tower has overhanging machicolations through which he and his servants could drop missiles on besiegers.

The Corbridge pele-tower is an early and well-preserved example of the characteristic Border towers built in response to the region's insecurity, which on the Scottish side of the frontier went on being built into the early seventeenth century. It is constructed of large, well-hewn stones quarried from the ruins of the nearby Roman fort of Corstopium. The pele is three storeys in height. The entrance door on the ground floor is of oak planks covered with an iron grate, and led into a vaulted basement where animals could be herded in emergencies. The first floor, probably the vicar's hall, has a number of medieval features – stone wall cupboards, window seats and a fireplace. The third floor has gone. The pele is now the Tourist Information Centre.

The adjacent parish church was largely reconstructed in the thirteenth century, apart from its Saxon tower: like the pele, the church was at least partly built with re-used Roman masonry.

Criccieth Castle stands on a rocky promontory jutting into Cardigan Bay. Constricted by its site, it is much the smallest of Edward I's north Welsh castles, and unlike the rest was not entirely a new building. For its irregularly-shaped grey stone outer walls, following the line of the hilltop, are those of an earlier native fortress, probably raised by the Welsh prince Llywelyn the Great (1200–1240). Occupied by Edward's forces in 1283, this stronghold was thereafter adopted as one of the chain of coastal fortresses intended to sustain English rule over the mountainous hinterland of Snowdonia: and between 1285 and about 1292 a new inner ward was built in a reddish stone, whose most distinctive feature is the great gatehouse with its pair of massive and strongly projecting semi-circular towers. Further work was done under Edward II, but Criccieth seems always to have been overshadowed by its much more powerful neighbour at Harlech, and after its destruction by Owain Glyn Dŵr's rebels in 1404 it was never restored.

CRICCIETH CASTLE
Gwynedd
OS 123 SH 500377
The castle stands on the sandy south coast of the Lleyn peninsula in north-west Wales, on the A497 between Porthmadog and Pwllheli. Harlech castle is some fourteen miles to the south-east (via Maentwrog) and Caernarvon about eighteen miles north (via the A487).

CROWLAND Lincolnshire
OS 131 TF 242103
Crowland stands amid level Fenland, eight miles north of Peterborough (with its cathedral) via the A47 to Eye and then the A1073 northward: it can also be reached from the A1 (fourteen miles to the west) via the A16 through picturesque Stamford, turning onto the B1156 at Market Deeping.

The east end of the ruined abbey.

St Guthlac (675–714) was a nobleman of royal blood from Mercia (the Anglo-Saxon kingdom centred in the Midlands). From about the age of fifteen he went on the rampage as a warrior, pillaging the Welsh. But in his early twenties he became ashamed of his way of life and joined a monastery at Repton (Derbyshire): and two years later he left to become a hermit, making his home in an old burial mound in the Lincolnshire Fenlands. There he attained the holy life, though haunted by demons – some of whom were armed and spoke in Welsh. At the site of his cell a Benedictine monastery was founded in 716: Crowland Abbey became a well-endowed and honourable house, not least because it housed the shrine of St Guthlac. It was dissolved in 1539, but a fragment of the monastic church has survived, being used as the parish church. This is mainly the nave: the chancel has gone. The standing western parts show that it was built on a large scale:

41

Top, a fallen sculpture. Above, the west front of Crowland Abbey.

the twelfth-century nave and west front were substantially remodelled in the thirteenth and fifteenth centuries. The exterior of the west front has thirteenth-century work with sculptures of a high order.

In the pleasant little Fenland town there is a unique triangular bridge dating from the later fourteenth century. It was built at the junction of three streams, where the rivers Nene and Welland meet. The sculptured figure of Christ now on it may originally have adorned the abbey's west front.

The Hundred Years War

By the fourteenth century there remained (apart from the Channel Isles) only one fragment of the French lands ruled by the Angevin kings of England in the second half of the twelfth century – namely the duchy of Gascony in south-west France. To the English Crown, however, Gascony was an immensely valuable possession, for from its principal city, Bordeaux, a great flow of wine was shipped to the Channel ports and London, providing English kings with huge customs revenues. But there was a snag. They held Gascony as vassals of the much more powerful French kings, who used their overlordship to interfere in Gascon affairs and to coerce their English vassals into supporting their policies, threatening otherwise to confiscate the duchy. It was to resist such a confiscation by Philip VI of France in 1337 that Edward III was to invade France. Edward, moreover, also had a claim to the French Crown: in 1340 he assumed the title of King of France to provide sanction for his French supporters and in hopes of attracting more. It was a title that the British Monarchy gave up only in 1802.

The English strategy of launching quick-moving mounted raids deep into France was to reduce much of the countryside to misery: and the English infantry tactics of combining men-at-arms and longbowmen produced notable victories at Crécy (1346) and Poitiers (1356). In 1347 Edward captured the important port of Calais, which was to remain in English hands until 1558: and in 1360 he managed to make a peace settlement by which he received south-west France in full sovereignty. But Charles V of France repudiated this settlement a few years later, and in the war of 1369–75 Edward lost most of his gains. His successors down to Henry VIII were to pursue various of the claims he had put forward in France, but after the loss of Normandy and Gascony in the years 1450–53 they were never again to rule a province of France.

CROXDEN ABBEY
Staffordshire
OS 128 SK 065398

The abbey ruins are five miles north-west of Uttoxeter, and are best reached by taking the B5030 Uttoxeter-Rochester road, turning west at Rochester onto a minor road towards Hollington, and then north onto a signposted road which cuts through the abbey. Two miles north of Croxden are the pretty Churnet Valley and the various attractions of Alton Towers.

Bertram de Verdun, lord of Alton, was an example of a new type of careerist found in twelfth century England – he was both layman and bureaucrat. He was a baron of that awesome and ingenious governmental novelty, the Exchequer, and a royal judge. Like many landowners who lived in Henry II's empire, (which stretched from Ireland to the Pyrenees) his culture was French. In 1176 he gave land to the Norman abbey of Aunay-sur-Odon, and the Cistercians of Aunay founded a new house, whose site at Croxden in the Dove valley was consecrated in 1181. The new abbey prospered through endowments and sheep-farming in the thirteenth century. In this period the church was built, 240 feet long, with an aisled nave of eight bays, transepts, a crossing over the tower and apsidal presbytery with a chevet of five radiating chapels – an unusually elaborate east end for

one of the Order's normally simple churches. Only fragments of the church remain, the most complete being the south wall of the south transept and the west wall of the nave. These show that it was a church of unusual distinction. The west wall has, between stepped buttresses, a deeply recessed entrance arch around which are grouped three great lancet windows. The effect is one of profound strength combined with graceful simplicity. It is a fine expression of Cistercian ideals.

There are also remains of some of the monastic buildings, including the chapterhouse, parlour, undercroft of the dormitory and the lavatory block (reredorter). Like many monasteries, Croxden suffered a decline in prosperity in the fourteenth century, and never fully recovered prior to its dissolution in 1538.

DIRLETON CASTLE Lothian
OS 66 NT 516840

Dirleton is two miles west of North Berwick and some twenty miles east of Edinburgh, via the A1 and the A198 through Musselburgh and Gullane. The coastline hereabouts is beautiful: and five miles east of Dirleton, on a precipitous clifftop, stand the spectacular remains of medieval Tantallon Castle, well worth a visit.

In the twelfth century the lands of Dirleton were acquired by the Anglo-Norman house of de Vaux, one of the knightly families who came to Scotland under David I's patronage. To protect their barony, not far from the sea and the mainland route from Lothian to England, they maintained an earth and timber castle: and in the thirteenth century they rebuilt it with stone defences, whose large scale and imposing appearance reflect the agrarian wealth of the barony. The site chosen was a crag with rocky natural defences, especially towards the west. The curtain-wall followed the line of the hill top: there were four semi-circular and one rectangular tower projecting from it. Best preserved are the cluster of two semi-circular and one rectangular tower at the south-east corner. Their interiors, especially the Lord's Chamber on the first floor of the keep-like

principal tower, give a good impression of the domestic comfort to which the Vaux family aspired. The gatehouse, the eastern wall and adjacent domestic block are largely rebuildings by the Haliburton family, who acquired the barony by marriage in the later fourteenth century. They were succeeded in 1515 by the Ruthvens, who also made alterations.

On Edward I's invasion in 1298, Dirleton was the strongest of the East Lothian castles held against him. It was besieged by Anthony Bek, Bishop of Durham, whose men were disheartened by having to subsist only on locally foraged beans and peas. But Edward urged the besiegers on with a peremptory message: supply ships arrived, and Dirleton was taken, to be garrisoned by the English until 1311. Dismantling after its eventual recovery by the Scots may have necessitated the Haliburton reconstruction.

Direlton Castle is firmly based on a foundation of natural rock.

Dorchester-on-Thames is significant in the history of the conversion of the English to Christianity. Pope Honorious I sent Birinus as a missionary to Britain: he landed among the thoroughly pagan West Saxons and set to work among them. In 635 he baptised their king, Cynegils; who, with the approval of his overlord King Oswald of Northumbria, gave Dorchester to Birinus. It was the seat of a bishopric until after the Norman Conquest, when the headquarters of the diocese was transferred to Lincoln. In the south choir aisle of Dorchester Abbey is the modern shrine of St Birinus, incorporating a fragment of the medieval shrine destroyed at the Reformation. In 1170 a house of Augustinian canons was founded here: the present church was built for them. Their domestic buildings have disappeared, with the possible exception of the Old School House (now the museum), which may have been their guesthouse.

The abbey church is pleasantly situated on rising ground at one end of the High Street with a good view of the Thames valley: its exterior is plain, with a tower reconstructed in the seventeenth century. Inside it, the nave and transepts display some twelfth-century features. But the east end is substantially a rebuilding undertaken in various stages during the thirteenth and early fourteenth centuries, the choir being extended and the choir aisles added in about 1340. The south nave aisle was also added in the fourteenth century for the use of the parishioners. These lavish and ornate new eastern works may reflect the success of the cult of St Birinus, for whom a new shrine was provided in 1320. The tracery of the east window is delicately sculpted as a tree stemming from Jesse, in whose branches are Gabriel, the Magi and Christ: and there are also sculptures of a procession carrying St Birinus' relics. Much original stained glass survives, depicting saints, prophets, and the arms of Edward III's nobles, including those of his son Edward Prince of Wales (the Black Prince). Perhaps their offerings to St Birinus helped to pay for the window.

The church is rich in medieval furnishings, from the lead font with figures of the Apostles (*c.*1170) to the early sixteenth century choir stalls. Most notable among the monuments

DORCHESTER-ON-THAMES
Oxfordshire
OS 164 SU 579943
Dorchester-on-Thames (not to be confused with the county town of Dorset) is nine miles south-east of Oxford, via the A423 Henley road. There is much else of interest in this area, notably historic Wallingford four miles to the south of Dorchester, and secluded Ewelme (six miles to the south-east, via the A423 and a minor road through Benson) with its magnificent fifteenth century church and almshouses.

45

is a vigorously carved stone effigy of a mailed knight (c.1280). His figure is alert, flexed, mobile; he draws his sword, ready to swing round at an opponent. This swashbuckling knight of the period of Edward I's Welsh wars is unlike the stiff, prayerful, hierarchial effigies of knights which were later to become the fashion. there is also a unique brass to an Augustinian abbot, and an effigy in legal costume, probably of a royal judge, John Stonor (d.1354). He greatly augmented the fortunes of his family, a leading knightly family in south Oxfordshire. Their descendant, Lord Camoys, still lives in nearby Stonor.

Dorchester's High Street has fine eighteenth-century facades, some fronting older structures, one example being the George Inn of c.1500, a coaching inn with a carriage entrance to its courtyard.

The effigy of Sir John Holcomb in Dorchester Abbey, the mailed knight drawing his sword.

DORNOCH CATHEDRAL
Highland
OS 21 NH 797897

Dornoch is on the far north-east coast of Scotland, some fifty-seven miles north-east of Inverness via the intermittently spectacular A9 road, which follows the coastline for much of the route.

Gilbert de Moravia (d.1224) received the bishopric of Caithness in the early 1220s. It was scarcely an enviable post, for the kings of Scots were only able to make their power felt intermittently in this disturbed region, which was part of the earldom of Orkney — indeed Gilbert's predecessor had been burnt to death by some of his flock; while the bishop before that had been blinded. Gilbert set up his bishop's seat at Dornoch, where there had been a cell of Dunfermline Abbey (Fife) before the mid-twelfth century: he constituted a chapter and also endowed the building of a cathedral. In accordance with the modest resources of the diocese it is built on the scale of a large English parish church, rather than of the mighty cathedrals further south. The exterior is solid and plain in composition, with a massive central tower and a spire. Of St Gilbert's building works there remain the choir, central tower and transepts, forming a finely proportioned interior. In the nave is the tomb of Gilbert's brother Sir Richard, killed near Dornoch fighting Danes: his effigy is a vigorous knightly one, though much damaged.

It is fortunate that so much survives of the medieval cathedral, for in 1570 it was burnt in a clan feud between the MacKays of Strathnaver and the Murrays of Dornoch, and in 1605 much of it was blown down in a storm. Choir and transepts were repaired in 1616; the ruined nave was replaced in 1835–37.

Nearby is the Bishop's Palace, a turretted tower-house which is now part of a hotel.

The principal port for Channel crossings to France, Dover is seventy-one miles south-east of London via the A2 and M2. The massive castle complex, towering above the harbour and accessible via Castle Hill Road, is well worth half a day's exploration: and a tour of its underground passages (summer only) is particularly recommended. Less than ten miles to the north (via the A258) are Deal and Walmer Castles, well preserved examples of Henry VIII's coastal forts: and Canterbury is also within easy reach.

Constable's Tower.

From prehistoric times the clifftop heights occupied by Dover castle have been a key defensive position. There was an Iron Age fortress here; and there are remains of a Roman lighthouse (Pharos), dating probably from the first century A.D. Adjacent to it is the Anglo-Saxon church of St Mary-in-Castro, dating from the late tenth or early eleventh century: this probably served the inhabitants of a Saxon defensive "burh". In 1066 William the Conqueror had a castle built here, and its defences were transformed by Henry II, who spent a fortune to turn it into one of the strongest fortresses in the realm, with the most modern defence system in Western Europe. He had some stone fortifications built here in 1168–74, but the main works date from the 1180s. Work on the great rectangular keep was well advanced by 1185; the architect was apparently Maurice "the engineer", who may have already designed the surviving keep at the royal castle of Newcastle-upon-Tyne. A bailey was constructed round the keep by a curtain wall defended by rectangular projecting towers, two pairs of which form the King's Gate to the north and the Palace Gate to the south. Both of these had barbicans with walls enclosing considerable sections of the inner bailey's wall, the northern one of which survives – they are in some ways similar to the later barbicans at *Conwy* Castle.

What is even more remarkably precocious is that an outer concentric curtain wall was planned – Dover is the precursor of the "Edwardian" castles in Wales in this respect.

It is not clear how much of this wall round the outer bailey was built in Henry's reign, but it was continued, with horsehoe-shaped towers, in his son John's reign: in 1205–14 over £1,000 was spent on the castle.

In 1215 John provoked civil war by repudiating Magna Carta: his opponents supported the French king's son Louis, who invaded the realm in 1216 and besieged Hubert de Burgh in Dover Castle. The siege was a failure, but came perilously close to success. The barbican to the northern gate of the outer bailey was captured and one of the towers of the gate was brought down by mining. But the garrison rallied to defend the gap and plugged it with timber. In the period 1217–56, therefore, about £7,500 was spent on works at the castle. The breached northern gate was blocked up and stengthened with additional defences, and a new gate was made to the west, the awesomely powerful Constable's Tower. This great tower is of two storeys, with the constable's hall and chamber on the first floor. The main block has flanking towers and one jutting forward from it: even if attackers managed to cross the drawbridge gap and penetrate this forward tower, they were still barred from the main gate by a portcullis.

Dover's medieval domestic buildings – and the defences – have undergone considerable alterations as a result of the continuous military occupation of the castle up to 1958, and the castle was extensively refortified against the French in the eighteenth and nineteenth centuries.

Part of Dover's Town Hall (in Biggin

47

Street) is a hall with undercroft dating from the thirteenth century. The adjacent tower (c.1221) was part of the Maison Dieu, a hospice for the infirm and for the pilgrims who flocked through Dover on their way to the shrine of St Thomas of Canterbury. The tower was built as a pious act by Hubert de Burgh, Earl of Kent, defender of Dover Castle, and subsequently domineering chief minister to the young Henry III.

Part of the curtain wall of Dover Castle.

DRUM CASTLE Grampian
OS 38 NJ 796005
Drum Castle is near Peterculter, some ten miles south-east of Aberdeen via the A93 and a signposted minor road turning northwards.

The castle, on a hill in what was once the royal Forest of Drum, is an early Scottish example of a tower-house: perhaps indeed the earliest, since it dates probably from the later thirteenth century. In 1323–24 Robert I made grants of the property to his armour-bearer William de Irwin. The Irvines, William's descendants, are an example of the families whose landed fortunes took off through their support of the Bruce cause. In 1640 the castle was briefly but spiritedly defended against a Covenanting force by the wife of Sir Alexander Irvine: the Irvines were firmly Royalists.

The granite tower has a formidable defensive appearance. It is rectangular with rounded corners, and the walls, at least twelve feet thick, rise seventy-six feet to a battlemented parapet walk. The windows, for security, are small and high up. There are three storeys: the original entrance was to the hall on the first floor, from which one set of stairs leads upwards, while another leads down to the ground-floor storage basement where there is a well. The adjoining mansion was put up in 1619. The Irvines still live in the castle.

DUNKELD Tayside
OS 53 NO 024426
The tiny cathedral city of Dunkeld stands in the beautifully wooded Tay valley, on the A9 midway between Perth and Pitlochry: by the entrance to the cathedral is "Old Dunkeld", a street of typically Scots seventeenth century houses preserved by the National Trust for Scotland. Immediately south of the city is Macbeth's Birnam Wood: and to the north-east (beyond Pitlochry) are the Pass and battlefield of Killiecrankie (1689), with an interesting Visitor Centre, and Blair Atholl Castle.

There was a flourishing monastery at Dunkeld when, in 850, the Scottish king Kenneth mac Alpin is alleged to have had the remains of St Columba brought here from the island of Iona to protect them from Viking raids. The old bishopric was revived early in the twelfth century, and the existing aisleless choir of four bays (now the parish church) dates in part from the thirteenth century, though it was extensively rebuilt by Bishop William Sinclair. This supporter of Robert the Bruce was a fighting bishop. In 1316 or 1317 he defended Auchtertool, a Fife manor of the bishop, against an English invasion force. Seizing a lance, he rode off in armour to do battle with the English, crying "Whoever loves his lord and his country, follow me!": the invaders were driven back to their boats. The headless ecclesiastical effigy in the church may be from Sinclair's tomb: and it also contains a monument reputed to be that of Robert II's son Alexander Stewart, a great man in these parts. He rejoiced in his nickname "the wolf of Badenoch", and his most infamous exploit (accompanied, as a Lowland chronicler says, by "wild, wicked Highlandmen") was to burn Elgin Cathedral in 1390.

The ruined nave, the chapter-house, the south porch and the tower all date from the fifteeenth century. The incident for which Dunkeld is most famous, however, took place after the end of the medieval period – in August 1689, when a single regiment of Covenanting "Cameronians" doggedly and successfully defended town and cathedral against a vastly superior force of Jacobite Highlanders.

Dunstaffnage castle stands on a rock at the tip of a promontory jutting out into Loch Etive. It commands an anchorage at the junction of land routes through the Grampian passes and sea routes to Morvern, the Isles of Mull and Tiree and the western seaboard. On this strategic site the Dalriada Scots established a fortress during the Dark Ages, but the present stone fortifications date from the second quarter of the thirteenth century. A curtain wall surrounds a roughly rectangular courtyard, with two round angle towers (which lack the projection characteristic of later "Edwardian" castles) and a gatehouse which originally had a drawbridge. The gatehouse has been drastically altered and the domestic buildings still standing in the courtyard are largely post-medieval. Near the castle are the remains of a thirteenth-century chapel.

Dunstaffnage Castle has a stirring history. It was built as a centre of their power by the Mac Dougalls, lords of the mainland region of Lorn and of the neighbouring islands, such as Lismore, Mull and Tiree. The Mac Dougalls were as up-to-date in their piety as in their fortifications – in c.1230 they founded the Valliscausian house, Ardchattan Priory, near Lock Etive. The family lost their lordship of Lorn as a result of opposition to Robert the Bruce: and in 1308 Robert defeated John Mac Dougall at the Pass of Brander, pursued the fugitives to the castle, took its surrender and garrisoned it.

Dunstaffnage then passed into the hands of the Campbells. In 1470 James III granted it to Colin Campbell, first Earl of Argyll: and in 1502 the second earl confirmed its custody to Alexander Campbell Keir, whose descendants, "the Captains of Dunstaffnage", still hold it. In the sixteenth and seventeenth centuries the castle was often a base for operations against clans opposing the Crown or the Campbells, such as the Macdonalds. As a Campbell fortress it was a centre of Covenanting power in the seventeenth century; in 1652–60 it was under English occupation. The Hanoverian interest held it in strength during the Jacobite rebellions of 1715 and 1745, an in 1746 the famous Flora Mac-Donald, who helped "Bonnie Prince Charlie" to escape "over the sea to Skye", was held prisoner here.

See **Pluscarden**

DUNSTAFFNAGE CASTLE

Strathclyde
OS 49 NM 883345

The ancient castle stands on a headland by the Firth of Lorn, just over three miles north of Oban via the A85 and a signposted minor road turning north at Dunbeg. Nearby is Dunollie Castle, another MacDougall fortress, on the coast just north of Oban (852315).

The Barony of Embleton was forfeited to the Crown by the treason of Simon de Montfort and granted by Henry III to his own son Edmund Crouchback, Earl of Lancaster. Edmund's son Thomas Earl of Lancaster, Edward II's cousin, was the greatest magnate in the realm and the king's fiercest critic, eventually suffering death in 1322 as a result of his intractability. At the height of his power, during the years between 1313 and 1316, Earl Thomas had a big new castle built in his barony of Embleton, on the coast at Dunstanburgh. Perhaps he built it to protect his property against Scottish raids, in the justifiable fear that Edward II's policies heralded disaster for Northumberland.

The site chosen was an isolated outcrop of the Great Whin Sill, a plateau of about eleven acres. Three sides of this are enclosed by the remains of Thomas's curtain wall and towers: the fourth did not need to be fortified – for it is a sheer drop of nearly a hundred feet down a basalt cliff into the North Sea. Combined with the natural surroundings, the gaunt remains of the castle make a dramatic skyline. The most impressive fragment and the main defence is the gatehouse, with its twin semi-circular towers. This gave access to a small inner ward, the residence of the owner and his household: the vast outer ward could be used as a refuge for the inhabitants and livestock of the barony. When John of Gaunt, Duke of Lancaster, the castle's owner, visited it in 1380, he thought the main gateway vulnerable: so he had it blocked up and devised a tortuous entry system beside it, leading only to the outer ward. The castle does indeed seem to have been an effective defence for the barony in these years of frequent raiding. The Scots tended to leave it alone: and Gaunt only had to worry in case the constable did not send down prime Northumberland salmon for his table.

During one phase of the Wars of the Roses, Dunstanburgh and other Northumberland castles became a strategic flashpoint. Henry VI's diehard supporters grimly hung on to them as a last remote refuge on English soil. But Warwick "the Kingmaker", Edward IV's lieutenant, took the surrender of Dunstanburgh in 1462 and again in 1464. The castle seems to have been badly damaged during these two sieges, and under the Tudors the Crown allowed it to fall into decay.

The castle is reached by a bracing walk along the cliffs from the fishing village of Craster, from which it was cut off in the Middle Ages by an inlet of the sea. The nearby village of Embleton is worth visiting. Its parish church has thirteenth and fourteenth century features, and part of the vicarage beside it is a fourteenth century vicar's pele.

See **Corbridge, Elsing, Monmouth**

DUNSTANBURGH CASTLE

Northumberland
OS 75 NU 258220

The castle stands on the Northumberland coast, eight miles north-east of Alnwick – which has its own large and well-preserved castle and interesting town defences: it may be reached from the main A1 either via the B1340 and a minor road to Craster, or via the B6347 to Embleton. From either Craster or Embleton a walk of around two miles takes the traveller to Dunstanburgh, which is inaccessible by car.

The ruined nave of Holyrood Abbey.

EDINBURGH Lothian
OS 66 NT 250736

Edinburgh, the capital of Scotland and undoubtedly one of the most beautiful cities in Britain, is 378 miles north of London. The map reference is to Holyrood Abbey and Palace, which stand in parkland at the foot of Arthur's Seat, and are due east of the spectacular Castle Rock (255735) via the Royal Mile, St Giles's Cathedral, and the Canongate. Craigmillar Castle (286708) three miles south-east of the city centre and just off the A68, is also well worth a visit: and Edinburgh boasts many interesting museums and galleries, notably the National Museum of Antiquities in Queen Street and the National Gallery of Scotland in famous Princes Street.

The most notable medieval remains in the beautiful city of Edinburgh are those of Holyrood Abbey, an Augustinian house founded by David I in 1128: its name stems from devotion to the True Cross of "Holy Rood", a strong cult among the west European aristocracies in the first flush of the crusading era. Canons came from Merton Priory (Surrey), and the abbey was well-endowed: David granted the monks the right to "build a certain burgh (town) between their church and my burgh". This was the Canongate, under separate jurisdiction from the royal burgh of Edinburgh. The latter was separated from the Canongate by a gateway, the Netherbow Port, whose position is marked on the road in the High Street (known as the Royal Mile). Kings often stayed in the abbey guesthouse and held councils there; and David II (d.1371) was the first of several kings to be buried in the abbey church. In the early sixteenth century James IV built a residence for himself west of the monastic buildings, but the earliest surviving part of this Holyrood House is the north-west tower built by his son James V in 1529–32. Charles II commenced the building of the rest of the existing palace in 1671 (the architect being Robert Mylne) and Holyrood House remains the monarch of Britain's chief official residence in Scotland.

Almost all that is left standing of the monastery is the nave of the church. When the Presbyterian General Assembly of the Kirk of Scotland ordered the church to be cast down in 1569, they allowed the nave to remain in use as the parish church of the Canongate. Major repairs to it were carried out under Charles I and Charles II; Charles I was crowned there in 1633 and it became the Chapel Royal. But on the overthrow of James VII in 1688, the chapel was ransacked by an anti-Catholic mob, and its roof collapsed in 1768. What is now left is the roofless nave, with aisles, and one of the two towers attached to the west front. The nave was part of a rebuilding which has been dated stylistically as *c.*1195–*c.*1230: its scale is imposing, and the beauty of the design and quality of the sculpture are to be judged against the best international examples. The western and eastern windows are seventeenth century insertions. There is one happy survival of the church's Pre-Reformation furnishings – the curious result of English vandalism: for in the parish church of St Stephen at St Albans (Hertfordshire) is a fine brass eagle lectern given to Holyrood Abbey in 1522, and probably looted by the English during one of their invasions in the 1540s.

Apart from the remarkable fragment of the abbey church, the historic town of Edinburgh is not conspicuous for its medieval buildings, except for the Romanesque St Margaret's Chapel at Edinburgh Castle and St Giles's Church in the High Street, an important example of a later medieval civic church. At the castle David II's fourteenth century Tower is concealed within the Half Moon Bastion, and a sad fragment of Trinity College Church, founded by James II's queen Mary of Guelders, is hidden away in Chalmers Close off the High Street, not its original location. The modern city has also swallowed up within its boundaries several fine medieval buildings – notably the splendid later medieval Craigmillar Castle and the collegiate churches of Corstorphine and Restalrig. However, the Old Town does have a great deal to interest the student of the Middle Ages – for the High Street, its closes, and the streets to the south of it preserve much of the pattern of the medieval town: while the high-storeyed houses of the High Street, though post-medieval, probably convey something of its atmosphere.

The parish church of St Mary, St Catherine and All Saints is a large cruciform building, with central tower, transepts, aisles and porch. It is immediately clear that it is a complete composition – an attractive one, whose projecting sections form complementary rectangular blocks. A feeling of strength and solidity is thus created – though the church was built in a world suddenly experiencing psychological and economic turmoil as a result of the Black Death of 1348–9. The character of the man responsible for having the church rebuilt appears only in his building works, here and at *Winchester Cathedral*: otherwise he is a faceless bureaucrat. William Edington (d.1366), presumably born here, was in Edward III's service by 1341 and was

his treasurer from 1345 to 1356. In 1346 Edward got the Pope to appoint him to the bishopric of Winchester, one of the richest English sees, and this enabled Edington to indulge his taste for building. In 1351 he founded a chantry for two priests in Edington parish church, but later changed his plans, transferring the foundation to an order of Augustinian canons, the Bonshommes ("good men"), who had only one other house in England. A new monastic foundation was then unusual. The new church Edington had erected for the canons was consecrated in 1361 – the year when plague once more ravaged England.

In the new church, the established Decorated style was modified by the strongly

EDINGTON Wiltshire
OS 184 ST 926533
Edington is on the northern edge of Salisbury Plain, three and a half miles east of Westbury by the B3098. Nearby is the site of King Alfred's great victory over the invading Danes in 898, which is perhaps commemorated by the great Westbury White Horse cut into the hillside above Bratton (898516).

The Beckington tomb in the south transept.

51

linear features of the new style favoured at court, Perpendicular. The interior has fine sculptured details including (a rare survival from Reformation iconoclasm) two statues in niches. There is medieval stained glass, notably a Crucifixion in the east window of the north transept: within, too, are three tombs of fourteenth-century knights (two with effigies) and the effigy of one of the canons wearing his robes, his feet resting on a barrel (or "tun" – probably a pun on his name). These contrast with a Renaissance monument to Sir Edward Lewys (d.1630) and his wife.

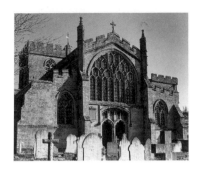

ELSING Norfolk
OS 133 TG 056162
Elsing is four and a half miles north-east of East Dereham and ten miles north-west of Norwich, via the A47 and a minor road turning north at North Tuddenham.

The brass of Sir Hugh Hastings.

The parish church of St Mary was rebuilt in c.1330 by the manorial lord Sir Hugh Hastings (d.1347), a rich landowner with exalted kinsmen. It is little changed: there is even a fragment of the original stained glass, a figure of the Virgin, in the south window of the chancel. The fourteenth century font and the fifteenth century font cover and screen are noteworthy.

But the outstanding feature at Elsing is Sir Hugh's brass, one of the most elegant and delicately engraved in England. He stands in the slightly mobile, swaying pose favoured by courtly artists. Above and around him flutter saints and angels and, on either side, in columns of niches, are the figures of princely and noble patrons echoing his pose. At the top, to Sir Hugh's right, is Edward III; to the left is Henry, the blind earl of Lancaster, whom Sir Hugh appointed an executor of his will. Henry's elder brother Earl Thomas had been executed for rebellion against Edward II in 1322, but Sir Hugh's last years were a happier time for Lancastrian retainers. Earl Thomas, lying in his tomb at Pontefract (Yorkshire) was more edifyingly occupied in performing miracles: while Earl Henry was firmly in Edward III's favour. And in 1347 the king himself was at a peak of success: he had just won the battle of Crecy and was about to gain Calais. Soon, however, the Black Death was to strike terror in his kingdom.

Elsing Hall dates from c.1460–70, but its appearance has been drastically altered.

The Black Death

Towards the end of the thirteenth century a subsistence crisis arose, for agricultural technology had not advanced sufficiently to solve the problem of overcropping on the poorer lands which had recently been taken into cultivation. In years of lean harvests the less well-off starved, and dearth and mortality were general in the terrible years of 1315–17, when harvests failed throughout Europe. These problems of subsistence were to receive a terrible solution, for the plague pandemic reached England in 1348 and Scotland the following year, and there were further outbreaks in 1361–2 and 1379–80.

Plague is a disease afflicting wild rodents. *Pasteurella pestis*, a non-mobile bacillus, multiplies in the rat flea which, when crammed with bacilli to the point of indigestion, kills the host rat by regurgitating them into the blood stream. When the rat dies, the flea bites humans or other available animals: "blocked" fleas can remain alive and infectious for up to fifty days without food. Bacilli, discharged into the blood through the flea's bites and faeces, cause a swelling or "bubo" in the lymphatic glands (in the groin, armpit and neck) which drains the infected limbs. The plague toxins produce high fever, coma, heart failure, inflammation of the spleen or kidneys, and sometimes destruction of tissue and consequent internal haemorrhage. The mortality rate in bubonic cases untreated by modern medicine is 60–85%, death occurring on average after five days of illness. Since the bacilli are normally active when the temperature is between 15° and 24°C (60° and 75°F), bubonic epidemics break out in warm weather, though when the rat population is heavily infected plague may persist in winter. In a septicaemic attack, the number of bacilli transferred to the host is so high that the victim invariably dies of blood poisoning, often within a day. In contrast to the bubonic and septicaemic varieties, spread only by rat fleas or the infected human flea, pneumonic plague is spread by human droplet contagion, and is one of the most virulent of all diseases. Pneumonic plague flourishes in winter weather, when humans suffering from colds are likely to be infectious.

During the medieval plague outbreaks men were at a loss to explain its causes or to prescribe effective treatment. Some writers explained that there was a corruption of the air induced by astrological conjunctions; others resorted to a theological explanation, seeing the misery as a manifestation of the divine wrath. Isolation of victims and burning of their effects were among measures taken to stop contagion.

Chroniclers, perhaps exaggerating, imply that over half the population of England died in the pandemic of 1348–9: and it is very likely that, especially in more densely populated regions of Britain, the pandemics really did cause steep declines in population, though there is evidence of some recoveries. This catastrophic plague had important economic and social effects: it led to changing relations between lord and peasant, a weakening of social ties and habitual patterns of behaviour within peasant society, and a restructuring of the pattern of rural settlement.

EXETER Devon
OS 192 SX 922925

Exeter is 172 miles south-west of London via the M4 and M5. The cathedral is in the town centre, and immediately east of the close are the High Street, containing the Guildhall; and Fore Street, off which are the Norman church of St Mary Arches and the well-preserved domestic buildings of St Nicholas' Priory (in the Mint). The ruins of Rougemont Castle are to to the north of the cathedral, in Castle Street: and to the north of it (on the Quay) is Exeter's famous and fascinating Maritime Museum, containing more than a hundred craft from all over the world, from a dugout canoe to a three-masted sailing barque.

Though Exeter had a monastery by the seventh century, it did not become the seat of a bishop until 1050: and the earliest surviving parts of the present cathedral, the unusual towers over the transepts, flanking the junction of nave and choir, were completed in about 1160. A chapter house for the cathedral clergy was begun in around 1225, and thereafter the whole church was rebuilt, beginning at the east end in the later thirteenth century and ending with the reconstruction of the west front under Bishop Grandisson (1327–69). Thus the present cathedral is essentially the work of the period from c. 1270 to c.1370: and it has some of the best sculpture in England of that period, not least on some of its many tombs.

The west front is the most notable exterior feature. It has a large central window with diminishing side arcades, and the lower part of the main facade is partly covered by a stone screen filled with two rows of statuary, the largest array of late medieval figure sculpture in Britain. On stylistic grounds the figures of kings in the lower range have been dated to c.1340–50, the figures in the upper range to the fifteenth century.

The nave has fine fourteenth century ribbed vaulting with an array of carved corbels and roof boxes. Above the north arcade is the famous minstrels' gallery (c.1360), fronted by fourteen stone angels playing musical instruments. The choir screen, with three low-centred arches offset by the arcade overhead, dates from c.1324, and the choir itself has a fine collection of roof bosses and misericord carvings (c.1230–70), though the medieval choir stalls have disappeared. The oaken bishop's throne, whose canopy is fifty-nine feet high, dates from c.1313–16; it is one of the great achievements of fourteenth century English design and carving: also notable are the sedilia in the presbytery (c.1320).

Exeter was an important strategic centre, the key to control of the West Country. The Romans built a fortress on the site, on the high ground commanding the crossing of the river Exe: it was the terminus of one of their great roads, the Fosse Way. The Roman defences were strengthened in late Anglo-Saxon times to make Exeter a fortified *burh*,

capable of resisting the Danes. Thereafter it was to be frequently besieged: and it was difficult to take. In 1068 its citizens defied William the Conqueror, only submitting after he had besieged it for eighteen days. He considered it worth maintaining undamaged, and negotiated generous terms: but immediately ordered his sheriff of Devon to build a castle there to secure and overawe the city. Rougemont Castle is in the northern corner of the Roman walls; there are remains of its stone outer walls and early gate. In 1136 King Stephen vainly besieged city and castle for three months; Baldwin de Redvers held it for his rival Matilda. Stephen, a considerable soldier, tried scaling, bombardment, and mining, but the garrison only surrendered when their well ran dry: the furious king wanted to make a horrible example of the defenders, but his barons dissuaded him and they were allowed to march out honourably. Then, in 1487, Cornish rebels supporting the Yorkist pretender Perkin Warbeck besieged the city, mounting violent assaults on the East and North Gates: but the citizens valiantly assisted the Earl of Devon and the local gentry in the defence. When the rebels fired the gates, the defenders banked up the blaze to drive them back and dug new ditches on the inside of the gates, and the rebels eventually withdrew with heavy casualties.

In 1086 Exeter was a prosperous place with a royal mint, a centre of regional trade. Later, however, it was to have difficult relations with the local magnate family, the Earls of Devon, because of the obstructions to navigation which they erected in the Exe and their attempts to divert trade from the city for their own profit. In the twelfth and thirteenth centuries Exeter had a flourishing weaving industry, and its rich mercantile élite prospered by exporting wool: while in the fourteenth century the rise of a rural cloth industry in the West Country gave Exeter merchants a major export commodity to make up for the declining overseas demand for English wool. Medieval Exeter suffered badly from bombing in the 1939–45 War, but retains some notable medieval buildings, such as the Guildhall, St Nicholas' Priory and St Mary Steps Church.

FLINT CASTLE Clwyd
OS 117 SJ 247734

The castle stands on the Dee Estuary, eleven miles north-east of historic Chester via the A549, the A55, and the A5119. There are a number of other castles in this much fought-over region, notably little Ewloe (288675) just north of the A55 and Hawarden (309653) just south of the road.

Flint Castle was the scene of one of the most melancholy occasions in the history of medieval English kingship – there, in 1399, Richard II became the prisoner of his rebellious cousin Henry of Lancaster, soon to usurp the throne as Henry IV (see Shakespeare's *King Richard II*, act 3, scene 3). The building of the castle was commenced by Edward I in 1277 during his invasion of North Wales, and was completed by 1280: the site chosen was a red sandstone promontory lapped to the north and east by the river Dee. At the same time as it was being built, ditches were dug nearby to mark out the site

of a new borough to be populated by English settlers. The grid plan of modern Flint derives from the medieval division of the town into blocks.

The castle consisted of an inner and outer bailey: a stone-walled causeway led from it to the town. The only visible remains of the outer bailey are its earthen ramparts: the site is occupied by a gaol built in 1785. The inner bailey is a rectangular enclosure, remains of whose curtain walls and three round corner towers still stand, though its domestic buildings have disappeared. But the most remarkable feature of the castle is the Great Tower,

The tallest remaining structure at Flint Castle is the north-east tower.

a large, round, independent keep outside the south-west corner of the inner bailey. This Great Tower had its own moat, reached by a drawbridge from the inner bailey, and commanded the separate entrance from the outer to the inner bailey.

The Great Tower could also be defended when the rest of the castle had fallen. It is composed of two concentric shells: the gallery between them in the basement has embrasures with arrow slits. There were two upper floors (the topmost now missing) which were probably the residence of the constable of the castle, and the tower had its own

well. A near continental parallel to the Great Tower is the Tour de Constance at the port of Aigues Mortes in Provence, whose well-preserved fortifications were built in the thirteenth-century: and it is probably no coincidence that, in 1270, before he became king, Edward I had sailed from Aigues Mortes on his crusade to the Holy Land. In 1283 Llywelyn ap Gruffydd, Prince of Wales, and his brother Dafydd rebelled against Edward's overlordship and besieged Flint Castle, but failed to capture it. It was dismantled in 1646, after a siege by the Parliamentary forces during the Civil War.

Framlingham is twenty-two miles north-east of Ipswich, via the A12 and the B1116 turning north at Wickham Market: the magnificent castle and equally fine church stand close together on the northern edge of the picturesque small town.

In 1100 or 1101 Henry I gave Framlingham to Roger Bigod, and he probably built a castle of earth and wood on rising ground by the river Ore, whose defences are marked by the ditches round the present outer and inner courts (or baileys). In 1175–77 the castle's defences were dismantled on Henry II's orders, but towards the end of the twelfth century another Roger Bigod, earl of Norfolk, added a smaller bailey (the Lower Court) on the west side and surrounded the roughly oval inner court with a stone curtain wall, studded with thirteen rectangular towers. This 'curtain wall castle', without a keep, is an early example in the medieval west of ideas about fortification brought back from the Byzantine Empire and the Middle East by crusaders. The earl's fortifications still stand, giving an awesome impression. The entrance gate, to the south, was modified in the 1530s, when the bridge was also probably built, and the ornamental brick chimneys on the towers. There were two postern gates, to the west and south. The latter illustrates the new sophistication of the military architect, for it leads to an elaborate projecting defence work, a fortified bridge ending in a tower on the outer rim of the moat. From this tower the approaches to the inner court could be covered in an arc reaching from the western postern to the main gateway.

Little remains of the castle's main domestic buildings, which were in this inner court. Here lived some of the most important people in East Anglia – and in the realm. The Bigod line died out in 1306, and six years later Edward II gave Framlingham to his half-brother Thomas of Brotherton, whom he made earl of Norfolk. From Thomas it

eventually passed to the Mowbrays, whose line failed in 1476, when a prominent Norfolk knight, John Howard, inherited the property. In 1483 he was tempted to support Richard Duke of Gloucester's bid for the throne in return for the Duchy of Norfolk: this "Jockey of Norfolk" died fighting for Richard III at Bosworth in 1485. But the Howards soon ingratiated themselves with the Tudors, from whom they would receive both great favours and harsh blows. Edward VI gave the castle to his sister Mary, and there she rallied the local gentry in 1553 against the attempt to put Jane Grey on the throne, riding thence triumphantly to London, eager to restore the Catholic Faith. The Howards finally disposed of the castle in 1635. It soon came into the hands of Pembroke College, Cambridge, on condition that they built the almshouse which still occupies the site of the medieval great hall in the inner court.

The large later medieval parish church has an impressive wooden nave roof, and fine tombs with Renaissance ornament. One of them is of Henry Fitz Roy, bastard son of Henry VIII and Catherine of Aragon's lady-in-waiting Bessie Blount. Loaded with nominal honours, including the title of Duke of Richmond, and married to the Duke of Norfolk's daughter Mary, Fitz Roy died in 1536, aged seventeen. His body, meanly wrapped in lead and lying on straw in a cart, was taken to Thetford Priory for burial near his Howard relations, and was moved here at the Reformation. Here also lies Thomas Howard, third Duke of Norfolk (d.1554), who won the great victory of Flodden against the Scots in 1513: the helmet he wore during the battle hangs near the high altar.

Framlingham's 'curtain wall castle' is an early example in this country of this particular form of fortification.

In November 1290 Edward I's beloved Queen Eleanor of Castile died near Lincoln, and her embalmed body was carried in sad procession to Westminster Abbey for burial. To mark his affection for his wife – and at the same time to enhance the prestige of the English monarchy by a display of its wealth and patronage of the arts – Edward afterwards raised elaborately sculptured memorials at each of the twelve places where the funeral cortège had rested. Three of these "Eleanor Crosses" survive, at Geddington and Hardingstone in Northamptonshire and at Waltham Cross in Hertfordshire: and of these probably the best-preserved and most original is the cross at Geddington. Basically triangular in shape, its lower stages are embossed all over with embroidery-like square and diamond shapes, and hung with the Queen's heraldic devices: while above stand three statues of Eleanor herself, beneath canopies which merge with graceful pinnacles forming the shape of a six-pointed star.

Statues of Queen Eleanor stand within her cross at Geddington.

GEDDINGTON ELEANOR CROSS Northamptonshire
OS 141 SP 896830
The cross stands at the centre of Geddington village, which is some four miles north of Kettering and just off the A43: the village's interesting medieval church contains fine fourteenth century carving and remnants of Saxon work. Four miles to the west is Rushton Hall, with its curious and delightful Elizabethan Triangular Lodge (SP 830831).

Glasgow Cathedral is the most impressive remaining medieval church in Scotland. Though its exterior is disappointing, in scale and in the majesty of its interior it ranks with better-known English cathedrals. It stands on a very early Christian site. Here, probably, the Briton St Ninian consecrated a cemetery towards the end of the fourth century, and here St Kentigern (alias Mungo) meaning "dear friend" set up a monastery and probably a bishopric in the late sixth century kingdom of Strathclyde. Kentigern was born into a royal dynasty in a British kingdom in Lothian, and was educated in Pictland, at Culross (Fife), by a hermit named St Serf. Kentigern fixed on Glasgow, according to later legend, because it was the place where two oxen halted which were pulling a cart containing the body of a hermit, Fergus, whom Kentigern intended to bury. Robert Blacader (d.1508), first Archbishop of Glasgow, may have had the southern crypt (known as the Fergus or Blacader Aisle) built to house Fergus's shrine: on its vault is a carving of the hermit's body on his cart.

In the twelfth century the bishopric was revived by endowments from David I and his successors, and a new cathedral was con-secrated in 1136. By the later part of the century it had an establishment of a dean and secular canons, and a new eastern extension was consecrated in 1197. But little twelfth century work is to be seen, for new building was undertaken on a lavish scale from the 1230s onwards. Taking advantage of the fact that the ground sloped, a two-tier east end was built, with a spacious crypt, whose design and sculptural details rate highly. The nave was rebuilt in the fourteenth century, and the choir screen, central tower, Blacader's Aisle and the remodelling of the two-storeyed chapter-house exemplify the Scottish vernacular style of the later Middle Ages.

In the crypt there is the place where St Kentigern's shrine stood from the 1420s, round which pilgrims processed; there is also a headless stone effigy, probably of Bishop Robert Wishart of Glasgow (d.1316), one of the principal opponents of Edward I and supporters of Robert Bruce. He was released from captivity in England after Robert I's victory at Bannockburn in 1314 and returned to his see, aged and nearly blind.

In Cathedral Square stands Provand's Lordship, a house built for a priest in 1471, and now a museum.

GLASGOW CATHEDRAL Strathclyde
OS 64 NS 604656
The fine (though frequently underestimated) city of Glasgow is 397 miles north-west of London and forty-four miles west of Edinburgh via the M8 motorway: the cathedral stands in a prominent position near the city centre, just off the A8 and not far from Queen Street station. Glasgow also has several exceptionally distinguished galleries, including the City Art Gallery and Museum in Kelvingrove Park (paintings, arms and armour) and the new Burrell Collection Building, Pollok Park (with outstanding medieval tapestries, stained glass and sculptures).

GLASTONBURY Somerset
OS 183 ST 501388

Much beloved by mystics of all kinds, Glastonbury is some twenty-five miles south of Bristol (via the A37 and A39) and five miles south-east of Wells and its cathedral. The abbey ruins are in the town centre, near the Abbots Tribunal in the High Street (499390) and the George Hotel : and legend-haunted Glastonbury Tor is just to the east, towering above the surrounding marshlands.

In the Middle Ages the legend became current that Joseph of Arimathaea had founded a church in Glastonbury, a few years after the death of Christ. The place in fact was very probably a cult centre connected with various early Celtic holy men, and the Anglo-Saxon king, Ine of Wessex, apparently founded a monastery there at the beginning of the eighth century. St Dunstan, born nearby, became its abbot in about 946 : he is said to have had a famous encounter with the Devil ; and the tongs with which he caught the Devil by the nose became a treasured possession of the monks. More historically, he carried out a model reform of the community, enforcing the Benedictine Rule. The confidant of the kings of Wessex, now the dominant power in much of Britain, Dunstan procured from them endowments and the nucleus of the abbey's fabulous relic collection. Several of these first Saxon kings of England were buried in its church, and in Domesday Book (1086), the abbey's listed possessions in Somerset add up to one eighth of the estates recorded in the shire. After a terrible fire in 1184, a complete and ambitious rebuilding of the church was undertaken : it was carried on over a long period, but substantially completed in the fourteenth century. Little is still standing, but fragments of the central crossing dating from the twelfth century indicate

its huge scale ; so does the distance away from these of the ruinous St Mary's Chapel, completed in 1187, which once stood at the west end of the church. This has richly decorated Romanesque arches, notably the Biblical scenes on the surrounds of the north and south doors.

There is little left of the monastic buildings, except for the superb and well-preserved Abbot's Kitchen, dating from the fourteenth century, one of the best examples anywhere of a medieval magnate's kitchen. In the High Street are two buildings connected with the abbey, essentially of the fifteenth century. They are the Abbot's Tribunal, where his court exercised a wide jurisdiction over his tenants, and the pilgrims' hostel, now The George Hotel. The parish churches of St John and St Benedict are good examples of characteristically stately Somerset churches dating from the later Middle Ages. Glastonbury Tor, a dominating hill, is crowned by the tower of a thirteenth century church, the rest of which has disappeared. On this hill Richard Whiting, the aged, ailing and confused last abbot, was hanged with two of his monks for treason by Henry VIII in 1539 : St John's church posesses some of his abbatial vestments. Of the abbey's great relic collection, only the spine from the Crown of Thorns remains (now in private possession).

The ruined eastern piers of the Abbey tower and, right, the well-preserved Abbot's Kitchen.

59

Gloucester is 109 miles north-west of London via the M40 and A40, and can be reached from the north or south-west via the nearby M5 (exits 11 and 12). The cathedral, clearly visible from the by-pass, stands to the north-west of the city centre, off Westgate Street – where Bishop Hooper's Lodging is now a folk museum: and a short walk takes the traveller to the Cross, the junction of Northgate, Southgate, Eastgate and Westgate Streets which has been Gloucester's focus since Roman times.

The tomb and effigy of Edward II in the north ambulatory of Gloucester Cathedral.

Gloucester occupies an important strategic position, at the point where the river Severn can easily be crossed on the road from London to South Wales. It was an urban centre under the Romans and the Anglo-Saxon Kings of Mercia, and William the Conqueror had a castle built there (which has disappeared): while he was staying in Gloucester at Christmas 1085 he ordered the Domesday Survey to be made. Medieval

Gloucester burgeoned as a centre for metal-working, using charcoal and iron from the nearby Forest of Dean: it also acted as a market for these commodities, as well as for the internationally prized wool from the Cotswolds and the cloth woven from it. Its prosperity was reflected in the number of its churches, giving rise to the saying "as sure as God's at Gloucester".

The Benedictine monastery there, re-founded in the early eleventh century, shared in this prosperity; the monks sold great quantities of wool from their Cotswold estates – hence their ability to build so magnificently. A new church was begun in 1058; and a replacement was dedicated in 1100 and completed in c.1160, much of the fabric of which stands. In it was buried Robert Duke of Normandy (d.1134), the least unattractive of William the Conqueror's three sons. He took part in the First Crusade and the capture of Jerusalem, having pawned his duchy to his brother William Rufus: his subsequent attempts to recover Normandy from his other brother Henry I led to his blinding and imprisonment for life in Cardiff Castle. His tomb, dating from the fifteenth century, is in the presbytery: on it is a vigorously posed wooden effigy of the tragic duke, moustachioed and in chain mail. This figure may date from c.1160, and is the only surviving medieval effigy of a member of the Norman ducal house.

The Norman abbey church (now the cathedral) is best seen in the nave, with its high round pillars and narrow triforia. The ribbed vault was added in 1245 and the two western bays were rebuilt in c.1420, when the west front was completely altered. The eastern parts of the church were remodelled in the fourteenth century: tracery in the new Perpendicular style, with its emphasis on rectangular panels, was superimposed on the Norman structure. The earliest part of the church remodelled in the new style was the south transept (c.1331–35); and its pièce de resistance is the choir and presbytery, where the clean lines of the Perpendicular arcades lead up to the busily elaborate ribbed vault. But the most startling feature of the Perpendicular work is the slightly bowed east window, one of the largest surviving medieval windows in Britain. It contains original glass and was probably intended to commemorate the souls of participants in Edward III's victory at Crécy (1346). The principal subject of the window is the Coronation of the Virgin, and in the lower tiers are figures of contemporary nobles. The choir stalls, of c.1350, have a fine series of misericord carvings.

The north transept was also remodelled in the fourteenth century; while the Lady Chapel was built in the later fifteenth century, and has original glass in its east window. In the north ambulatory is the tomb of Edward II. After his probably violent death in *Berkeley Castle* in 1327, his body was eventually buried in the abbey, and a magnificent tomb was built – here we have not just a king's tomb, but the shrine of a saint, popularly if not papally canonised, which escaped destruction at the Reformation because of his royal status and probably because of the unofficial and minor nature of the cult. Yet in the fourteenth century Edward's body had acquired a reputation for miracle-working, and his descendant Richard II (d.1400) came on pilgrimage to it and tried to procure official canonisation. The alabaster effigy of Edward is an idealised realisation of holy kingship, far removed from the petty, petulant reality: above it is a finely sculpted canopy, whose curved arches contrast with diagonal buttresses and vertical finials.

The central tower of the abbey church was built in c.1450. Some of the conventual buildings survive, including the chapter-house and the impressive cloisters, whose east walk has the earliest surviving fan vault in England (c.1351–64). After the dissolution of the monastery its church became in 1541 the cathedral of the new diocese of Gloucester. In 1555, during the reign of the Catholic Mary Tudor, the Protestant Bishop Hooper was martyred outside St Mary's Gate: he is supposed to have spent his last night in the house known as Bishop Hooper's Lodgings in Westgate Street. God's presence is now not so apparent in Gloucester: but there are remains of St Oswald's Priory, (the Blackfriars), and there is the church of St Mary de Crypt in Southgate Street. The New Inn in Northgate Street is one of the finest examples of a half-timbered inn built round a courtyard.
See **Berkeley Castle**

The manor of Great Coxwell belonged to Beaulieu Abbey in Hampshire, a Cistercian house founded by King John: Court House Farm, dating from the late seventeenth century, is probably on the site of the monastic grange. Adjoining it is a most impressive medieval barn, mainly of stone construction and dating from the thirteenth or fourteenth century. It is $152\frac{1}{2}$ feet long and fifty-one feet high, and roofed with stone slats. It has a projecting "transept" in the centre of each side, and the interior has other similarities with a church: it is aisled by oak posts standing on square piers.

The parish church dates mainly from the twelfth and thirteenth centuries: the western tower was added in the fifteenth century. One of the brasses in the nave is of William Morys "sumtyme fermer of Cokyswell" (c.1500). He was presumably the tenant farmer, living in the grange and leasing the manor from the abbey.

GREAT COXWELL Oxfordshire
OS 163 SU 269940
Great Coxwell is some twenty-five miles south-east of Oxford, immediately south-east of Faringdon and just off the A420. The Great Barn (National Trust property) is north of the village, and is open from April until October.

Monks and Chroniclers

The medieval monk was devoted to the performance of the *Opus Dei* or "work of God", the daily – and nightly – celebration of the liturgies with his brethren. Monks lived subject to the Rule of St Benedict (d.550), or to one of the variations of it observed by the new religious orders which sprang up in the late eleventh and early twelfth centuries. Benedict of Nursia had enacted that monks should live as a community under the authority of their father abbot: they were to sleep in one dormitory, eat in one refectory and share other domestic facilities; and they were to take vows of chastity, poverty and obedience. Benedict laid down (with humanity) how this rule was to be enforced, what the diet of monks should be, and their daily timetable. A new development in monasticism from the tenth century onwards was the monastic Order – a scattering of monasteries, in some cases all over Western Europe, under the authority of one or more mother-house, forming a single congregation under direct papal authority and outside the control of the local bishop and magnates. This was the model developed by Cluny Abbey in Burgundy and its "Cluniac" cells, which was to be copied and refined by the new reformed congregations, above all that of Cîteaux (the Cistercians).

We know about the common framework of monastic life from monastic Rules and the ground-plans of monasteries, and about back-slidings and attempts to reform. Rare monastic biographies, like Walter Daniel's life of Ailred, Abbot of Rievaulx (which reflects the first flush of Cistercian fervour in Yorkshire) also reveal something of the mentality of particular monks. But this is hard to get at; and generally the individual monk remains faceless. Some shafts of light, however, appear in monks' literary compositions. Benedict had enjoined that they should study: and the copying and illumination of manuscripts and the composition of treatises, mostly of a religious character, became traditional monastic occupations. Monks were particularly interested in copying histories, which illuminated the unfolding of the divine will. Sometimes they added information about contemporary events, but generally they wrote history in the rather stilted form of annals – accounts of what happened year by year.

The most prolific monkish chronicler in medieval Britain was Matthew Paris (d.1259). He composed a huge "Greater Chronicle" (*Chronica maiora*) and, with unusual originality, produced different editions of this, mainly on a smaller scale. His works were popular: copies were made for different monastic libraries, and we are lucky to have some autograph manuscripts, a rare survival. Paris was a monk of St Albans Abbey, one of the oldest and richest Benedictine houses in England – an independent monastery with its own daughter-houses, whose Anglo-Saxon foundation predated the development of religious orders. The monastery stood on the hill where Alban, the first Christian martyr in Britain, was beheaded during the persecution of the Emperor Diocletian; it overlooked the ruins of the Roman city of Verulanium, and outside its gates the medieval town grew up under its control. The great Romanesque abbey church, with its ungainly plastered columns of plundered Roman bricks, is now the cathedral: it houses remains of the shrine of St Alban. This was a favourite place of pilgrimage, within easy reach of London and on one of the principal routes northwards. Great men often stayed in its guesthouse: and consequently Paris was not cut off from the secular world in his cloister, but exceptionally well-informed about national and international affairs. He knew leading personalities of the day from Henry III (whom he did not like) downwards.

Paris's chronicles tell us much about his world-picture and his personality. His world was one in which western Christendom was at the height of its expansion. Men who were westerners ("Franks") by origin and culture ruled (if somewhat precariously) in Constantinople and other parts of Greece, and in parts of Syria, Palestine and Asia Minor. Paris knew a great deal, therefore, about what was going on in the Eastern Mediterranean. He was also passionately interested in the affairs of the two institutions which dominated the West – the papacy and the Holy Roman Empire. He avidly followed the attempts of Emperor Frederick II to impose his rule in Italy and the counter-attempts of popes to reduce and destroy Imperial power. Thus we can see from Paris's attitudes and interests that some well-educated men living in thirteenth century Hertfordshire had a fuller sense of belonging to a European polity than perhaps ever before or since: they would, however, have talked in terms of Christendom, not Europe.

Yet, paradoxically, Paris was extremely insular in his outlook – and his virulent hatred and contempt for foreigners shows how the Anglo-Norman aristocracy, especially after King John's loss of his and their possessions in northern France during the early 1200s, were developing a sense of Englishness. Paris's denunciations of all sorts of foreigners as in various ways reprehensible and disgusting demonstrate that he was an intemperate, hysterical man, indiscriminate in his use of evidence, unreflectively seizing on anything which supported his prejudices. But above all he denounced the papacy – so fiercely that Matthew Parker, Elizabeth I's first Archbishop of Canterbury, re-published some of his works as Protestant propaganda. Paris's animus against the papacy – which led him to forge discreditable material – shows how papal government of the Church was becoming so efficient and authoritarian that it was alienating the clergy: the alliance between papacy and clerical élites which had done so much for the reform of the Church was fraying.

Matthew Paris is therefore an unreliable historian, but his work is invaluable as a reflection of contemporary attitudes, and gives insights into preoccupations in the cloister. Paris was a conventionally devout man: if his fellow monks were like him, they were fiercely proud of their house and willing to defend its interests blindly. But he and they were perhaps men who were not able to detach themselves from the secular world as Benedict wished. They might adhere to his Rule (though some abbots were lenient in granting dispensations from it), but they found the drama of the secular world too absorbing.

GREAT YARMOUTH Norfolk
OS 134 TG 525075

Great Yarmouth is on the Norfolk coast, nineteen miles east of Norwich via the A47: remains of the town defences appear principally in the quay area, and nearby are the Greyfriars Cloisters (525073) and two preserved houses in the Rows (525072) with displays of local furniture. These are open on weekdays from April to September only. Four miles north of Yarmouth is Caister, with an unusual fifteenth century "water-castle" (504123).

Great Yarmouth was built on a spit of land between the North Sea and the river Yare: its prosperity in the early Middle Ages arose principally from its proximity to the rich herring-fishing grounds and to an East Anglian hinterland which was one of the most populous and prosperous parts of the realm. Yarmouth also profited from being an out-port of one of the biggest medieval English provincial cities, Norwich. But above all it benefited from medieval folk's insatiable appetite for fish, stimulated by the many days of abstention from meat ordained by the Church, above all the long forty-day Lenten fast. Yarmouth's annual fair became the principal English market for herring and the town fought "herring wars" with the Cinque Ports in the thirteenth century. In the following century Yarmouth was in conflict with Norwich over tolls charged on the latter's exports, and with the port of Lowestoft over Yarmouth's attempt to control the herring catch at the haven of Kirkley Road – the harbour at Yarmouth was silting up. But the burgesses' monopolisation of the sale of an item of staple diet angered both the common folk of the town and the people of the surrounding countryside, and in the Peasants' Revolt of 1381 an attack on the town was headed by a local knight, Roger Bacon of Baconsthorpe. In the fifteenth century Yarmouth's prosperity apparently slumped, for reasons not now clear.

Yarmouth was protected from sea assault by stone walls which stretched from the river Bure in the north to the river Yare in the south, where a tower (no longer existing) controlled a boom restricting access to the river docks from the sea. Taxes (murage) were raised in the later thirteenth century for the construction of the walls, and work was done on them in the 1330s and 1340s, when danger of assault by the French was added to the normal one of incursions by North Sea pirates. Much of the walls remain, with eleven of their thirteen original towers, but their ten gates have disappeared. The quay area by the Yare and the alleys behind it ("the Rows") preserve something of their medieval form, though most of the buildings are post-medieval. There are scanty remains of a friary in Greyfriars Way. The parish church of St Nicholas, much rebuilt in the later twelfth and thirteenth centuries, is notable for its large size: it was heavily restored in the nineteenth century and after the Second World War.
See **Rye**

HADDON HALL Derbyshire
OS 119 SK 235664

This fine house is set among wooded hills just off the A6, two miles south of Bakewell and six and a half miles north-west of Matlock: it is open from Tuesday to Saturday during April to September only. Five miles to the north-east is another stately home, the massive Classical palace of Chatsworth (open daily, late March–October) which presents an interesting contrast with Haddon Hall.

Medieval Derbyshire was not particularly restful. It had its untamed hill country, and in some respects it was regarded as part of the North of England, whose inhabitants were viewed with wariness by southerners. The gentry were particularly unruly. In 1438, according to Professor R. L. Storey, one of them called Peter Venables was said to have taken to the wilds, living there with his band by robbery "like as it had been Robin Hood and his men": and in 1455 the sheriff complained of heavy expenses incurred through "riding with much people on his own costs in executing of his office, because the people is wild". The Vernons of Haddon, long-established locally and one of the leading Derbyshire gentry families, were certainly capable of wildness too. They were licensed to fortify their house at Haddon in 1195, and Haddon Hall was to become one of the largest and most complete medieval country houses in England, with features dating from the twelfth to the seventeenth centuries. It was a fortified house, but alterations from the fourteenth century onwards were concerned with enhancing domestic comforts.

Haddon Hall is divided into an Upper and a Lower Courtyard by a set of apartments built in about 1370, consisting of hall, kitchen, parlour and, above the last, a solar. These give a very full impression of the dwelling-place of a leading northern family, knightly in status, at the end of Edward III's reign. The hall screen dates from c.1450, its panelling from c.1600; the gallery is sixteenth century, and the parlour has its original painted ceiling of heraldic shields. The chapel was heavily remodelled in the fifteenth century, and is one of the best examples of a noble's domestic chapel from a period when the aristocracy were keen to embellish private worship in their households: it has fifteenth century wall paintings and stained glass. The scale and sumptuousness of the Vernons' buildings show that they were determined to live like lords and to display a sophistication equal to that of rich, disparaging southerners. Haddon Hall is one of the best surviving expressions of the wealth and aspirations of leading medieval gentlefolk – families whose political support magnates craved.

Haddon Hall also has noteworthy later features, such as the Long Gallery built in c.1600 by John Manners, whose descendant, the Duke of Rutland, still owns the Hall. There are fine seventeenth century gardens.

Harlech is the most spectacularly positioned and one of the strongest of the castles which Edward I built to hold down his conquests in North Wales. It is situated in a commanding position just south of the Lleyn Peninsula, near the northern end of Cardigan Bay. The crag on which it is built is over 200 feet high, and was originally lapped by the waters of Tremadog Bay (now land at this point), across which beacon signal communications could be maintained with *Criccieth* Castle. Work was begun on Harlech during Edward I's 1283 invasion and was virtually complete by 1289. The architect was James of St George: like his later castle on Anglesey, *Beaumaris*, it has two lines of parallel concentric fortifications. The core of the defences, within whose courtyard were the domestic buildings, is the rectangular inner bailey, with its massive corner drum towers and the horseshoe-shaped towers of the gatehouse, the latter projecting boldly inwards into the bailey as well as outwards: this gatehouse could be defended when all else had fallen. The inner bailey's defences tower over the parallel middle bailey's, whose gatehouse

(covered by fire from the inner bailey's) had a drawbridge over the moat which stretched from the east round to the south. The other two sides of the site are precipitous, but enclosed for a wide area by walls to form an inhospitable outer bailey, protecting access from the sea. There was a watergate, from which supplies had to be hauled agonisingly up a path running parallel to the castle wall, then circling to meet defensive obstacles before the postern was reached.

The castle (and its neighbour Criccieth) proved their worth to Edward I during the 1294–95 rebellion, when they held out despite having their land communications cut. In 1404 the garrison, reduced by starvation and disease, surrendered to Owain Glyn Dŵr, who put his family and treasure in the castle. But in 1408–9 the English (under the command of the future Henry V) returned and mounted a long siege. Mining and bombardment by artillery were in vain: only a blockade eventually induced surrender. The epic defence of Harlech, however, occurred during the Wars of the Roses. In 1461 Edward IV seized the throne and defeated his rival

HARLECH CASTLE Gwynedd
OS 124 SH 580314
Harlech stands on the west coast of Wales, between the sea and the Rhinogs mountain range and on the A496 between Barmouth and Porthmadog. This beautiful coastline is famous for its shells and its dunes, and it is worth visiting Llandanwg (two miles south) whose tiny ancient church is often half buried by shifting sands.

The massive gatehouse of Harlech Castle.

65

Henry VI in Yorkshire: Henry fled to Scotland, but in Wales his half-brother Jasper Tudor, Earl of Pembroke inspired Welsh Lancastrians to resist, especially at Harlech. A Londoner commented that "that castle is so strong that men said it was impossible to get it". In 1464 Edward gave his leading Welsh supporter Lord Herbert £2,000 costs to capture it: the master of the king's ordnance supplied artillery, yet the castle held out, only surrendering to another siege by Herbert in 1468, when the Yorkists were roused to make an exceptional effort by a lightning invasion of Wales under the diehard Lancastrian Jasper Tudor. In the sixteenth century the Crown allowed the castle to fall into decay. During the Civil War it was garrisoned for Charles I, and yet again this "castle of lost causes" suffered a long siege before it finally surrendered in 1647, the very last Royalist fortress in mainland Britain to fall to the Parliamentarians.

See **Beaumaris, Criccieth**

The gatehouse at Harlech seen from the inner courtyard.

HEXHAM Northumberland
OS 87 NY 935642

Hexham is some twenty miles west of Newcastle-upon-Tyne via the A69, and at the centre of an area of outstanding historical interest. Hadrian's Wall with its Roman forts is just to the north, Corbridge with its church and Vicar's pele is four miles to the east, and all around are Border tower houses like Aydon Castle.

Seen from the north, across the river Tyne, Hexham still has the air of the remote, isolated frontier town that it was in the Middle Ages: its houses huddle up a hill topped by two grim medieval towers as well as the priory church, now the parish church. It was the "capital" of the archbishop of York's liberty of Hexhamshire, over which his steward (not the king's sheriff in Northumberland) presided. The steward held his court in the Moot Hall, the large tower dating from the late fourteenth or early fifteenth century on the east side of the central Market Place. Not far behind the Moot Hall is the other tower, the Manor Office, built *c.*1332: this was the archbishop's prison, with its grim dungeon – one of the earliest custom-built prisons surviving in England.

Hexham Priory's origins go back to the early days of Christianity in the Anglo-Saxon kingdom of Northumbria. Wilfrid (634–709) was a Northumbrian nobleman, educated by Irish monks on Holy Island (Lindisfarne), who became a priest and soaked up Christian culture on his visits to Rome and Lyons. He was a combative man: he was deposed three times from his Northumbrian bishopric. The church he built at Hexham, probably modelled on a Roman basilica, is likely to have been destroyed with its monastery by Vikings in the ninth century, but a precious survival is the crypt of the present church, built of great stone blocks pillaged from buildings of the Roman frontier (Hadrian's Wall is not far away). Here, where the church's sacred relics were kept, one stands today in a dimly lit, hallowed spot, scarcely altered since Wilfrid's day. In the chancel there is a stone Anglo-Saxon bishop's chair, known as Wilfrid's Throne. The chancel and transepts (*c.*1180–1250) were part of an Augustinian house founded in 1113. The most remarkable remaining feature of this is the canons' night stair in the south transept. Up and down this the canons processed for centuries between the dormitory and the choir to chant their night office. The steps are very worn.

The church has interesting furnishings, such as the tombstone of the Roman cavalryman Flavinus (first century A.D.): triumphantly he rides dow a naked hairy Briton, crouched in submission. The chancel has fifteenth-century furnishings – rood-screen, choir stalls, and the chantry chapels of two priors. There is a wealth of wood-carving, and of undistinguished panel paintings of saints. Their survival is surprising, considering that Elizabeth's leading local frontier official, the cantakerous old Sir John Forster (Warden of the Middle March) made his home in the church. But generally, religious sentiment in Northumberland at that time remained strongly traditional.

This is an exceptionally well-preserved moated manor-house, built and extended for successive leading families among the medieval Kentish gentry. The house is built round a quadrangle: the earliest part, the eastern block, dates from the fourteenth century, and may have been built by Sir Thomas Cawne, whose armoured effigy (c.1373) is in Ightham parish church. The principal feature of the block is the hall, which has a high-pitched roof of open timber-work, (the wood panelling and mantel are nineteenth century). At the lower end two doors lead to the kitchen and buttery, and towards the upper end a door gives onto a staircase up to the solar and what was originally the chapel.

In the later fifteenth century the house belonged to the Haute family, whose fortunes were made by their kinship to Elizabeth Wydeville. She resisted the amorous advances of Edward IV (d.1483) and finally induced him to marry her. In his last years Edward made her cousin Sir Richard Haute a great man in Wales and a councillor of the heir to the throne; Haute's brother Sir William was sheriff of Kent when Edward died. But the Hautes were soon to lose Ightham.

In 1483, when accompanying the young Edward V from Ludlow to London, Sir Richard Haute was arrested by the king's uncle Richard Duke of Gloucester, imprisoned, and executed as one of the Wydeville faction. Later that year, not surprisingly, Sir Richard's son and his brother Sir William rebelled against Richard III. Under Henry VII the Hautes recovered Ightham, but their fortunes never revived; in about c.1509 the property was sold to Sir Richard Clement.

The Hautes may have built the gatehouse tower, inserted the five-light window in the hall and improved it with the luxury of a fireplace and chimney to replace an open hearth. Sir Richard Clement erected a new timber chapel on the north side of the quadrangle. It has fine interior woodwork, and the heraldic devices painted on the spaces between its rib vaults echo the relatively care-free atmosphere of the early years of Henry VIII's court, when the king was fond of his first wife and avidly pursued pleasure. Beside Clement's arms appear the mixed Tudor rose and the pomegranate of Aragon (for Queen Catherine) – devices also found in glass in the hall windows.

IGHTHAM MOTE Kent
OS 188 TQ 584534
Set among the wooded hills of the Kentish Weald, Ightham Mote is some six miles east of Sevenoaks, by the A25 and signposted roads turning south through Ightham Common and Ivy Hatch: Ightham church, with its fine collection of monuments, is in Ightham village, just over two miles north of the house at OS 594569. The house is open on Fridays only from February to November, and also on Sundays in summer. Nearby is thirteenth century Old Soar Manor, a mile east of Plaxtol (619541): and there are many other notable houses in the area – Knole three miles to the east, near Sevenoaks; and Hever Castle and Penshurst Place some ten miles to the south.

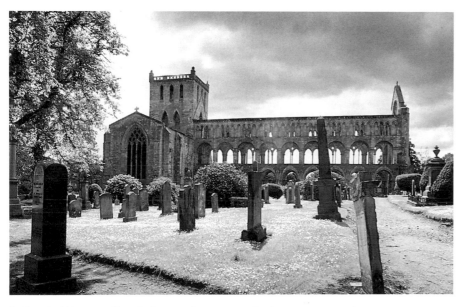

JEDBURGH Borders
OS 74 NT 650204
The border town of Jedburgh is some fifty-six miles south-east of Edinburgh, on the A68, the most picturesque route through the Borders. All around are wooded valleys and frontier tower houses, and to the north-east are two more fine abbeys, Dryburgh near St Boswells and magnificent Melrose.

The ruins of Jedburgh Abbey are uncommonly complete for a building of its great age.

Jedburgh Abbey was founded originally as a priory of Augustinian canons by David I in about 1138. The church stands out impressively on a hill overlooking the river Tweed, the monastic buildings terraced on the south-facing slope down towards the river. The church is roofless, but most of its walls stand to roof height, more or less as they were built for the canons in the twelfth and thirteenth centuries. The west front, reasonably intact, is a well-proportioned, uncluttered Romanesque composition, but the tower was reconstructed in 1504–8. The interior, especially the view eastwards down the nave, is beautiful, in glowing sandstone: it is noble in concept and scale, with tiers of arcades and some delicately sculptured capitals. The tower and transepts, dating from the twelfth century, are in the main Romanesque, though the nave has early Gothic arcading, as do the later extensions of the eastern parts. Here one can best experience the architectural triumphs that Border abbeys could attain in their early medieval heyday. Much can now be seen of the monastic buildings, which are currently the object of a major excavation.

After the Scottish Wars of Independence Jedburgh, so near the frontier, was precariously placed. The castle and neighbouring Jedforest were held by the Percies, the dominant English family in Northumberland, as part of the English enclave in Roxburghshire. But the Percies' rights were bitterly disputed by the leading Scottish Border family, the Earls of Douglas, and echoes of their bickering have reached us in ballads such as *Chevy Chase*. In 1409 the Scots finally expelled the English from Jedburgh. About the end of the century James IV (who died heroically at Flodden in 1513) founded a Franciscan Observant friary there – a reflec-

tion of reforming movement among the religious Orders, the greater interest of the Crown in Border affairs since the fall of the Douglases in 1455, and perhaps of more secure conditions in the region. The friary has recently been excavated and its considerable remains can be seen. The sixteenth century, however, was to be a period of renewed insecurity in the Borders, and it was then that "Mary Queen of Scots' House" was built in Jedburgh, a solidly defensive tower-house. The well-to-do then built themselves defensible stone houses in other Scottish Border towns, and this exceptionally well-preserved example is now a museum devoted to the queen.

The roofless nave of Jedburgh's abbey church.

In 1106 Henry I granted the lordship of Kidwelly to his minister Bishop Roger of Salisbury, and the bishop had the castle built to protect the lordship, at the point where the river Gwendraeth flows into the Towy, just inland from Carmarthen Bay. The fortress was entrusted to Maurice de Londres, but the hold of the Londres family was soon to be challenged by the resurgent power of the Welsh princes of Dynevor. The Lord Rhys captured the castle in 1190, and in the 1230s it was in the possession of Llywelyn ap Iorwerth. During the 1240s Patrick de Chaworth, husband of the Londres heiress, recovered it, and the castle and lordship later came to the House of Lancaster through the marriage in 1298 of the Chaworth heiress to Edmund Crouchback's son Henry, future Earl of Lancaster. In 1403 the castle was besieged by Owain Glyn Dŵr, and he attacked again in 1405, with a French force assisting: neither assault succeeded.

The castle consists of two wards, an inner one surrounded on three sides by an outer one. The oldest stone fortifications are those of the inner ward, possibly built by Payn de Chaworth c.1275: there a curtain wall encloses a rectangular area, with semi-circular towers at the corners. A new hall, solar, kitchen and chapel were added in about 1300. The outer ward was then given stone fortifications, including the castle's most prominent feature, the main gatehouse. This is rectangular, three storeys high, with two semi-circular towers flanking the gateway, and has a stone projection on the east side to give covering fire along the outer wall of the castle. This gatehouse may have been the constable's residence: on its first floor there is a hall and a kitchen with fireplace and oven, and the solar is on the top floor. The gatehouse, which could be defended when the rest of the castle had fallen, was extensively repaired after the Welsh and French tried to fire it in 1405.

The fortified town of Kidwelly lay immediately outside the castle: its main gateway, dating from the fourteenth century, is all that survives of its stone defences.
See **Elsing, Monmouth**

KIDWELLY Dyfed
OS 159 SN 409071
Kidwelly is on the south-west coast of Wales, midway between Carmarthen and Llanelli on the A484. Ten miles to the east, between Llanelli and Swansea, is the beautiful Gower Peninsula, an area of outstanding natural beauty.

The building of Kildrummy Castle was connected with the expansion of Scottish royal power into the north-east in the thirteenth century: it may have been raised by Gilbert de Moravia, Bishop of Caithness (d.1245), who looked to the protection of Alexander II. The castle was intended to secure control of a pass which led southwards from it through Mounth to Deeside, and northwards gave access to Speyside. It was later held by the Earls of Mar, and when Robert Bruce was defeated at Methven in 1306, he sent his wife and daughter across the Mounth to seek refuge in the castle. Soon afterwards, however, it was besieged by the Prince of Wales (the future Edward II) and the Earl of Pembroke, and surrendered after a traitor had set fire to the grain stored in the great hall.

The castle is protected by steep ravines on all sides. Its inner bailey has five sides: there are two circular towers at the northern corners of its curtain walls, the north-west one built on the scale of a keep. Two horseshoe-shaped towers project from the western and eastern walls and at the southern extremity is a strong rectangular gatehouse with semi-circular projecting towers – little remains of this gatehouse. All this stonework probably dates from the thirteenth century, and the overall design is of the mature thirteenth century sort found in major castles in England and Wales.
See **Dornoch**

KILDRUMMY CASTLE
Grampian
OS 37 NJ 455164
The castle is just south of Kildrummy village, which is thirty-seven miles west of Aberdeen and ten miles west of Alford, via the A944 and the A97.

LANGLEY CASTLE
Northumberland
OS 87 NY 825624

The castle is about eight miles west of Hexham, via the A69 and the A686 to Alston (which passes directly by it). It is surrounded by pleasant wooded countryside, and a few miles to the north, across Tynedale, is Roman Hadrian's Wall.

Langley Castle is first mentioned in 1365; it is a tower-house, but as befitted the head-quarters of a barony, it was built on a larger scale and with more distinction than the tower-houses of knights and other lesser aristocrats (compare *Balsay* and *Chipchase*). It has four impressive projecting corner towers: the south-western one being a remarkable toilet block, with rows of seats divided by stone walls on each floor, discharging through vaults at the foot of the tower into the castle ditch. Langley was designed to house a substantial garrison in emergencies: for it was on a main Scottish invasion route, leading to the Tyne valley and the bishopric of Durham.

The castle and lordship belonged to the Percy family, who held the earldom of Northumberland from 1377 onwards and were perhaps the most powerful magnate family in the English Borders during the later fourteenth century. But as a result of their growing embroilment in national politics they were to forfeit the castle. In 1405 it was taken by Henry IV's forces: the king was suppressing a revolt which had Percy backing, and had already demonstrated to the Borderers that he was as ruthless as they by having the Archbishop of York executed. Henry's health, however, was never the same afterwards. At the start of the Wars of the Roses the Percies showed that they had learnt fidelity to the Lancastrians by supporting Henry VI (Henry IV's grandson) against the Yorkist rebels. This turned out to be a mistake: the Percies had backed a loser. In 1464 the Lancastrians held out against Edward IV in Langley Castle and other Tynedale strongpoints, such as the Moot Hall in *Hexham*. But Warwick "the Kingmaker's" brother, John Neville Lord Montague, surprised and overwhelmed their forces near Hexham, bagging the Lancastrian leaders. Henry VI escaped, but had to leave behind his crown and armour, and Langley fell. Henry was captured next year in a wood in Lancashire, and was subsequently murdered in prison in 1471; there is hair matted in blood on his skull in St George's Chapel, Windsor Castle.

In 1470 the Percy heir had been restored to the earldom of Northumberland by Edward IV and had recovered Langley: but in 1541, when the castle was once more in the Crown's hands, it was reported that the roofs and floors were decayed and that only the walls were standing. It was restored and made habitable in the nineteenth century: that was when the present battlements were added.

LICHFIELD Staffordshire
OS 128 SK 115098

The small cathedral city of Lichfield stands to the north-east of the Birmingham–Wolverhampton conurbation, near the junction of two Roman roads, the A5 (Watling Street) and the A38 (Ryknild Street) to Burton and Derby. The cathedral and its fortified close are near the centre of the city, which is also famous for its associations with Dr Samuel "Dictionary" Johnson.

A church was built at Lichfield in about 700, to house the remains of St Chad (d.672), first bishop of the Midlands kingdom of Mercia. An imposing new church was built in the early twelfth century, but at the end of that century this was pulled down to make way for an even more imposing replacement, the present cathedral. The existing choir, presbytery, choir aisles and central tower were built in 1195–1208; and the chapel of St Chad's Head was added on the south side in about 1225, above a room which housed the bishop's consistory court. Between then and 1240 the transepts were built, and by 1249 the chapter-house was completed, outside the north wall of the choir. It had an upper storey which once housed the cathedral treasury but is now the library, whose most famous possession is the priceless Anglo-Saxon St Chad's Gospel Book. The nave was completed in 1285, and the west front, with its towers and spires in about 1320, while the Lady Chapel dates from c.1330.

Ann Kettle has described how the inhabitants of the medieval cathedral close formed a distinct community, physically separated from the city: for the close had a stone wall and moat, and two great gatehouses guarded the entrance; causeways linked the close with the city to the south. The cathedral and its close, however, were to pay a terrible price for their defensibility during the Civil War. The close was twice besieged by parliamentary forces: and the cathedral was bombarded, ransacked, garrisoned and wrecked so badly that most of it was left open to the sky. It underwent restorations after the Civil War and in the eighteenth and nineteenth centuries, but though ruthlessly stripped of its medieval fittings (its statuary, windows, woodwork and monuments) the original design remains surprisingly intact. Lichfield is notable as an English cathedral nearly all built in the classic thirteenth and early fourteenth century phases of Gothic architecture, and has great unity of design in pleasant red sandstone. The west front, with its bands of rich geometrical patterns offsetting statuary, gives an effect of compact restrained power: while the massive grouping of the three towers and spires has a dramatic effect unusual in English cathedral architecture.

The Vicars' Close has half-timbered medieval houses in which the vicars choral lived. The medieval city lay across the Minster Pool: it was founded by the bishops in the twelfth century and remained part of their manor of Longdon until the Reformation. It was a small place with little industry and only local trade. Modern Lichfield remains pleasantly small in scale: it has many eighteenth century buildings, and in the Market Square is the birthplace of Samuel Johnson.

Fortunes of War

By the fourteenth century the English Crown accepted that it had to pay daily wages to everyone from magnates downwards who served as soldiers on its expeditions to France and in its garrisons there, and elsewhere abroad. Peasants who could equip themselves as men-at-arms and archers were entitled to high rates of pay. They enrolled under the command of aristocratic captains of retinues, who had contracted with the Crown to lead a company and who received pay instalments from the Exchequer for themselves and their men. And though wages often fell into arrears as a result of the Crown's financial difficulties, there were also other possible sources of profit – plunder and ransoms. For the captor of a rich aristocrat had the chance of making a fortune, and while magnates and captains were obviously best placed to take important prisoners, there were opportunities for others to advance themselves socially through the chances of war. One such was Sir Robert Salle, a brutal man, quick to violence and no respecter of property. By 1372 he had such a high military reputation, gained presumably in the wars of France, that Edward III retained his services with a large annuity. But what was to make him most famous was the manner of his death in 1381. The leading chronicler of the day, Jean Froissart, describes how Salle was in Norwich when it was attacked by a band of rebel peasants. He rode out to confront them: but they tried to persuade him to join them, reminding him he too was born a villein. This made Salle very angry, and he abused the peasants so violently that they lynched him: English chroniclers mention his death with expressions of regret.

The late K. B. McFarlane provided corroboration for Froissart's story about Salle's alleged peasant origins: he discovered that Salle was the son of a mason from the Norfolk village of that name. So here we have an instance of a peasant's son who went off to be a soldier, and so distinguished himself and acquired so much profit that he was thought worthy and able to maintain the estate of knighthood. Though Salle was probably unusually successful, he is unlikely to have been the only peasant who improved his status in this way.

Upward social mobility was not new in English society. In the early twelfth century, for instance, Ranulph Flambard (Henry I's chief minister and Bishop of Durham) had originated as a humble link-boy. The Church thus offered advancement to those who showed administrative talent, while in the fourteenth century the law and administration were also developing as lay professions, and these probably provided more secure avenues for advancement than the lottery of war. The pen was more reliably profitable than the sword.

The historic city of Lincoln is 130 miles north of London, and is most easily reached by taking the A1 to Newark and then turning north-east on the A46, the Roman Fosse Way. The cathedral (visible for miles) and the neighbouring castle (which contains a chilling Victorian prison chapel) dominate the city from their hilltop, and here too is Bailgate with its fine period shop-fronts: nearby is the outstanding Museum of Lincolnshire Life in Burton Road. The lower town, reached by descending Steep Hill and the Strait (with their Jew's Houses) also contains notable buildings, including St Peter-at-Gowts church with its Saxon tower.

Wulfwig, the last Anglo-Saxon bishop of *Dorchester-on-Thames*, died in 1067. William the Conqueror preferred to have the seat of this bishopric at the other end of the huge diocese, in the troublesome north, where the bishop and the knights he owed for his barony would be of more strategic and political use. Lincoln was an important regional centre, at the junction of two Roman roads and connected to the sea by a network of waterways: so Wulfwig's successor, the Norman Bishop Remigius, transferred the headquarters of his diocese there and built a cruciform cathedral on the hill-top site of a Roman fort, which dominated the medieval town and the surrounding landscape. Here cathedral and royal castle formed enclaves side by side, jointly overawing the citizens and peasants below them, symbols and centres of the power of Church and State. The surviving parts of the Norman church are the grandiose and ostentatious west front, the lower tiers of the two western towers and the west bay of the nave. This church, consecrated in 1092, was in the twelfth century badly damaged by fire and some years later by an earthquake.

The work of reconstruction was initiated by a bishop whose holiness was to become a powerful stimulus to the glorious rebuilding of the cathedral in the thirteenth and early fourteenth centuries. Hugh of Avalon (1135?–1200), by origin a Burgundian nobleman, was a monk of the strict Carthusian Order who made a good impression on Henry II. Henry brought him to England to reform the Carthusian monastery at Witham (Somerset) and in 1186 procured the bishopric of Lincoln for the reluctant Hugh. As bishop he placed sanctity before conventionality and a quiet life. He had the deer in his park at Stow killed to feed the city poor, though venison was considered fit only for consumption by nobles. An episcopal swan at Stow displayed the sort of intimacy with him that birds and animals were to have with Francis of Assisi. The bishop was also an opponent of royal tyranny – he incurred Henry II's wrath by excommunicating an oppressive royal forester and Richard I's by opposing taxation. He was canonised in 1220 as St Hugh of Lincoln.

St Hugh's Choir (*c*.1200–10), with its distinctive Purbeck marble shafts, rib vaults and naturalistic carving, is a prime example in England of the new Gothic style. The iron screens are thirteenth century; the stone choir screen is fourteenth century, and so are the six canopied arches on the north side of the sanctuary: the three eastern ones contained the Easter Sepulchre, where the Host remained from Maundy Thursday until Easter Sunday. They have sculptures of foliage and sleeping soldiers. To the west of this arcade are the much restored remains of the tomb and chantry of Catherine Swynford (d.1403), for long the mistress of Edward III's son John of Gaunt, Duke of Lancaster (d.1399). Their liaison during his wife Con-

stance's lifetime gave widespread offence, and their marriage after Constance's death was a court scandal, because of the disparity in their birth. They were concerned to legitimise their children (surnamed Beaufort), one of whom, the future Cardinal Henry, became bishop of Lincoln in 1398. The Tudor dynasty descended from the Beauforts and derived their claim to the throne from this descent.

The cathedral nave was rebuilt in 1200–50 and the first two stages of the central tower were erected in 1235–53; the upper stage dates from the early fourteenth century. The canonisation of Bishop Hugh provided an incentive for the rebuilding of the eastern parts, to provide a setting worthy of his shrine. Here his remains were transferred in 1280 in the presence of Edward I and Queen Eleanor: the royal pair are represented by two carved heads behind the altar. The bosses of the vault in the retrochoir which housed St Hugh's shrine (known as the Angel Choir) have outstanding sculptures: angels are carved on them, some holding musical instruments, while one holds the sun and moon; and at the base of the foliated capital of the north-east pillar is carved the little creature known as the Lincoln Imp. The great east window has lost its medieval glass, but some remains in the window in the north transept known as the Dean's Eye (*c*.1210). The cathedral is also rich in medieval ecclesiastical and secular tombs.

Three sides of the cloisters remain; they have a wooden vault dating from 1296–1300. The chapter-house (*c*.1230–50) is an early example of a polygonal building; it contains an oak chair dating probably from Edward I's reign – a rare survival of medieval furniture. The Library contains one of the four early extant copies of Magna Carta. To the west of the cathedral is the fourteenth century Exchequer Gate, the entrance to the walled cathedral close, and to the south is the Bishop's Palace, parts of which are medieval.

To the west of the close is the castle, founded by William the Conqueror in 1068, and raised in the south-west corner of the Roman fort. A large irregularly shaped courtyard was surrounded by banks of earth, and a motte was raised as an insertion in the southern bank. The timber defences were later replaced by stone walls, of which there are remains, including the Lucy Tower on the motte: other prominent features of the stone defences which were developed and reinforced in the thirteenth century were the main gatehouse, facing the cathedral close, and the projecting horseshoe-shaped tower at the north-east corner, Cobb Hall.

The castle and cathedral are linked with the city below by the aptly named Steep Hill, which has some of the earliest remaining town houses in Britain, dating from the late twelfth century – Aaron the Jew's House and the Jew's House. Well-to-do Jews needed to build solid stone houses to safeguard their cash and bonds from fire, and themselves from assault – hence too their need for proximity to the castle and bishop's palace, so that they might seek the protection of royal and episcopal officers in emergencies. There was, indeed, violent anti-Jewish feeling in Lincoln in the twelfth and thirteenth centuries, which culminated in a wave of hysteria in 1255–56. Hugh, the son of a townswoman called Beatrice, was said to have been found dead in a well belonging to Copin, a Jew, and the citizens believed that the Jews of the city had ritually crucified the boy. Copin was arrested and forced to "confess" the crime. A blind woman was healed by touching Hugh's body, and he was buried in the cathedral, where his shrine became the centre of a cult. On Beatrice's plea, Henry III ordered Copin's execution, and other Lincoln Jews were also executed.

The city of Lincoln was one of the most prosperous in England in the twelfth and thirteenth centuries, though thereafter it declined. It had a weavers' gild in 1130, and it specialised in the production of high quality cloth; Lincoln greens and scarlets were justly famed. The centre of modern Lincoln retains something of its medieval character and fragments of its medieval buildings. Notable among them is the Greyfriars, Broadgate (now the City and County Museum), the earliest remaining Franciscan church in Britain: building commenced in 1237, and the church is remarkably well preserved. Another notable building, dating from the fifteenth and sixteenth centuries, is the Guildhall above the Stonebow Gate. It houses the Mote Bell, cast in 1371 to summon the city assembly; the civic regalia includes a sword given to the city by Richard II.

See **Dorchester-on-Thames**

LONDON
OS 176/177 TQ 337805

The Tower of London and Westminster Abbey stand respectively at the eastern and western extremities of medieval London, the Tower being most easily reached via Tower Hill underground station and the Abbey via Westminster station or by bus: alternatively, in summer, river boats ply between Tower and Westminster Piers, a pleasant twenty-minute journey. Southwark Cathedral, on the south bank of the Thames and within sight of the Tower, is immediately east of London Bridge main line and underground stations: and the Temple Church is in the heart of "legal London", in the lawyers' quarters called the Inner Temple. It is perhaps best reached via the underground to Aldwych, turning right outside the station and walking along the Strand (past St Clement Danes and the Law Courts) and Fleet Street until Chancery Lane is reached: immediately opposite Chancery Lane end is a narrow signposted passageway, leading directly from Fleet Street to the church.

Effigies of eight knights occupy the central nave of the circular Temple Church. An arcade of pointed arches lines the wall of the aisle beyond.

Many traces of medieval London remain, including the street names and street plan of the City and the dedications of its parish churches: but much of the old capital was destroyed by the Great Fire of London, perhaps the most grievous loss being Old St Paul's Cathedral, replaced after the conflagration by Sir Christopher Wren's famous domed church. Among the survivors, however, are two of the best known and most important buildings of medieval England, the Tower of London and Westminster Abbey: as well as two major churches of London's once-numerous religious orders, the Temple Church and Southwark Cathedral.

The Temple Church off Fleet Street – heavily restored after that other great assault on London, the bombing Blitz of 1941 – was built for the crusading order of the Knights Templar and consecrated in 1185. Its remarkable round nave, a frequent feature of Templar churches, is copied from that of the church of the Holy Sepulchre in Jerusalem, and is built in a Romanesque style which contrasts with the Gothic choir, completed by 1240. It contains early tomb effigies of famous Templars, including that of William the Marshal (d.1219), Earl of Pembroke and Regent of England.

Southwark Cathedral – south of London

Bridge, and thus in an area outside the jurisdiction of the medieval city – was the church of a house of Augustinian canons founded in 1106 and dissolved in 1539, whereafter the church became parochial: it was raised to cathedral status in 1905. This too has been heavily restored, especially the nave: but the choir, the complex arrangement of chapels at the east end, and the north transept are thirteenth century, while the south transept is fourteenth century. Against the north wall of the nave is the tomb and effigy of John Gower, poet and friend of Geoffrey Chaucer: he wears a chaplet of roses and the livery collar of his patron Henry IV. The nearby Harvard Chapel commemorates John Harvard, founder of the famous American university, who was christened in Southwark in 1607.

The Tower of London was the principal royal fortress protecting and overawing London. It was begun by William the Conqueror at the junction of the eastern section of the Roman city wall with the river Thames, covering the approach to the city and its one bridge: and his great stone keep, the White Tower (so called because it was whitewashed in the Middle Ages) remains remarkably intact. In the last decade of the twelfth century, stone walls enclosing a bailey round the White Tower were built on the east and river sides: the Bell Tower, at the south-west corner of the present Inner Ward, dates from this period. The castle was further strengthened and enlarged by Henry III and Edward I: and despite many alterations the Tower remains recognisably the fortress which existed in about 1300, with two concentric rings of much-altered walls and towers surrounding the White Tower. In the thirteenth century these defences were pushed out towards the city and the river, and beyond the Roman wall: and were surrounded by a moat, formidably wide on the landward side. The main entrance from the city (in the south-west corner) was covered by forward defences across the moat, leading to the Outer Ward's Byward Tower, with its twin projecting circular towers and portcullis. A watergate (called Traitor's Gate) projected from the Outer Ward, linked to a wharf on the other side of the moat: it has distinctive narrow round corner towers. Through this gate was the main entrance to the Inner Ward, protected in the thirteenth century by the large round Wakefield Tower, which now houses the Crown Jewels. The chapel off the main vaulted chamber in which they are kept is reputedly the scene of the murder of Henry VI in 1471. The gateway's defences were strengthened in Richard II's reign by the construction of the Bloody Tower, where the "Princes in the Tower" – Edward IV's young sons – are said to have been done to death in 1483.

In the fourteenth century the Tower was largely supplanted as a royal residence by Westminster Palace and suburban palaces such as those at Langley (Hertfordshire), Eltham (Kent) and Sheen (Richmond, Surrey). But the fortress continued to have a variety of important functions – as a prison, storehouse, manufactory of heavy weapons, record repository and menagerie. It was well maintained, and brought up to date as a stronghold by Henry VIII. It was garrisoned against attack in 1450, when Jack Cade's rebels seized the city; again in 1460, when Henry VI's partisans held out there for a while against the victorious Yorkists in the city; and yet again in 1471, when it was manned for Edward IV against the massed assault of Essex rebels.

Westminster Abbey was in existence by 970, but was rebuilt on a magnificent scale by Edward the Confessor, who lived just long enough to see the new church consecrated, and was buried there in 1066. Nothing now survives of his church, though some of the monastic buildings of the Norman Benedictine convent attached to it remain, namely the Chapel of the Pyx and the Undercroft (formerly a common-room under the monks' dormitory), both reached from the cloisters. The present abbey church is largely the result of Henry III's lavish patronage. Dogged by

rebellions from his youth, Henry greatly admired the French monarchy – which was richer and more stable than the English crown, and blessed by a variety of sacred associations, especially with St Denys and his great abbey near Paris. Henry therefore wished to have a magnificent church built at Westminster to honour its canonised founder the Confessor, and to emphasise the sanctity of the English monarchy at a time when he had to protect himself from restless subjects by strengthening the Tower. The foundation stone of the new church was laid in 1245, and within ten years the chancel, transepts and first bay of the nave were completed. By the 1260s four more bays were finished; and in 1269 the body of St Edward was translated to its present shrine. The church is aisled throughout, with an eastern ambulatory and radiating chapels in the French manner: its great height in relation to its width is also characteristic of cathedrals in the Ile de France, emphasising the fact that Henry sometimes felt more at home in Paris than in London.

Work on the nave was resumed in 1375, and Henry VII's Chapel at the east end was commenced in 1503. This houses the tomb of the king and his consort Elizabeth of York, with their splendid effigies by Pietro Torrigiano, but it was originally intended as the setting of another royal cult to exalt the monarchy from abasement – that of Henry VI, whom Henry VII tried to get canonised, and whose body he planned to bring there from St George's Chapel in Windsor Castle.

The Chapel of St Edward the Confessor is behind the High Altar: the original base of the saint's shrine remains, of Purbeck marble decorated with glass mosaic work. The oak coronation chair of Edward I, used at the crowning of every English sovereign, is also in the chapel: it contains what is alleged to be the Stone of Destiny, on which Scottish kings were anciently consecrated, and which Edward stole from Scone during the Wars of Independence. Henry III set a fashion for royal burials around the sides of the chapel. His gilt bronze effigy is one of the finest tomb sculptures in the abbey, and other notable memorials from the period are those of his half-brother William de Valence, of Edward I's queen Eleanor of Castile, and of Edward III and his queen Phillipa.

The abbey's chapter-house, dating from c.1245–53, is one of the largest in England, with a tiled floor of c.1355. During the later fourteenth century, on the occasions when parliaments met at Westminster, the knights of the shire and burgesses often held their sessions in this chapter-house, and sometimes in the abbey's refectory. In the Undercroft are some of the life-sized effigies which were carried in the funeral processions of royal and eminent personages. The earliest fragment is a head of Edward III which, from the contortion of the lips, may have been a death mask showing the effects of a stroke.

LONGTHORPE TOWER
Cambridgeshire
OS 142 TL 163983

The tower is just off the A47, two miles west of the cathedral city of Peterborough and some five miles east of the main A1 trunk road: the neighbouring village of Castor has a fine Norman church.

Longthorpe Tower's medieval portions were built by the Thorpe family, tenants of *Peterborough Abbey*, and were probably intended to mark the family's rise in the social scale to knightly status. The earliest part, which probably contained a hall, is likely to have been built in 1263–4 by Sir William Thorpe; while the great tower added to this wing's north-east corner was probably added in about 1300 by Robert Thorpe. There is also another wing, most of whose features are seventeenth century.

The Great Tower is a solid, rectangular structure of three storeys, with a battlemented parapet walk. The ground floor was probably for storage: entry to the first floor was through

a wall passage from the medieval wing. This floor was the Great Chamber, the lord's private apartments. There is another floor above this, with a garderobe in a small chamber in the south wall, which has a stone lavatory seat. The fourteenth century details in the Great Tower are well preserved.

What makes Longthorpe Tower wholly exceptional, however, is the preservation of the most complete set of domestic mural paintings surviving from medieval England, discovered beneath a coat of whitewash during the 1940s. They are painted on plaster on the walls of the Great Chamber of the tower, and have been dated to the second quarter of the fourteenth century. They are

76

of high quality, depicting Biblical, didactic and secular subjects: giving the impression of manuscript illuminations spread out on walls, they afford us a precious insight into the mental world of a medieval "gentry" family. The paintings also illustrate contemporary life. The Seven Ages of Man on the north wall has the Infant in a cradle; the Boy with a ball and whip; Manhood with hawk and lure; Old Age with his life savings in a bag; and Decrepitude on crutches. The artist was clearly fond of bird illustrations, including species found in the neighbouring Fenlands, such as bittern and curlew.
See **Peterborough Abbey.**

Left and above, some of the medieval paintings which decorate the walls of Longthorpe Tower.

Ludlow is built on a hill above a bend of the river Teme. The castle was founded near the end of the eleventh century either by Roger de Montgomery, Earl of Shrewsbury or by Roger de Lacy, both Norman lords establishing themselves in the Welsh borderlands. It has an inner bailey (one side of which overlooks the river) divided by ditches from the much larger outer bailey, whose defences were connected to those of the town lying beyond it. The fortifications of the inner bailey, the curtain walls, towers and four-storeyed keep (originally the main entrance from the outer bailey) date from the twelfth century, as does the unusual round chapel within the inner bailey, whose nave contains arcading with fine Romanesque mouldings. The outer bailey's stone walls also date from this century.

The reason why the castle received such impressive stone defences so early is to be found in a medieval ballad about the local Fitz Warin family. The ballad tells of the fights for possession of the castle between Marcher families, who persisted in exercising the right to conduct private warfare. The Lacys, who eventually established their claim to Ludlow, died out in the male line in 1240, and the heiress of their successors, the Genevilles, married Roger Mortimer of Wigmore, first Earl of March (d.1330).

The Mortimers were the most powerful family in the Marches of Wales during the fourteenth century. In the early part of it they built the splendid range of domestic buildings on the north side of the inner bailey, which constitute one of the best surviving examples of the residence of a medieval English magnate. In the fifteenth century the castle and lordship were inherited by the House of York – Richard Duke of York (d.1460), his sons the future Edward IV and Richard III, and Edward's sons, the ill-fated "Princes in the Tower" all lived here. So did Henry VII's short-lived son Arthur Prince of Wales, who

died in 1502 shortly after bringing his bride Catherine of Aragon here (his tomb is in Worcester Cathedral). In the sixteenth century and later the king's chief official in the region, the President of the Council in the Marches, had his official residence in the castle: in about 1581 President Sir Henry Sidney built the house beside the entrance to the inner bailey.

Ludlow's large parish church of St Laurence has fourteenth and fifteenth century features: it contains much medieval stained glass, and heraldic and anecdotal carvings beneath the misericords in the choir stalls. The church is also rich in Elizabethan and early seventeenth century monuments. The town itself is full of interesting old buildings, such as the partly medieval Reader's House near the church and the fifteenth century Guildhall of the Palmers' Gild in Mill Street. To the south of the town, Ludford Bridge dates from the same century, and it was here that one of the first encounters of the Wars of the Roses took place in 1459. Richard Duke of York, with his allies the Earl of Salisbury (his brother-in-law) and Salisbury's son, Warwick (to be known to posterity as "the Kingmaker") held the castle and town against Henry VI and a formidable array of lords. The Yorkists fired their guns at the royal army, but could not hold Ludford Bridge after a key company of professional soldiers deserted to the king. So York and his noble friends ignominiously deserted their men, leaving them to kneel for the king's mercy: York's wife, Duchess Cecily, was left behind too, to witness the sack of the castle.

The adjoining village of Ludford is also worth a visit, especially for its medieval parish church and for Ludford Hall, parts of which are late sixteenth or early seventeenth century.
See **Much Marcle.**

LUDLOW Shropshire
OS 137 SO 508745
The picturesque town of Ludlow is twenty-seven miles south of Shrewsbury via the A49, and on the eastern edge of the Welsh Border hill country. The castle stands on a cliff to the west of the town, and outside its gate is a maze of ancient streets (with many timber-framed houses, notably the Feathers Inn) surrounding St Laurence's church. Ludford village is immediately south of the town, across the Teme.

Holidays and Holy-days: the Medieval Parish

Parish church and churchyard, because they were sanctified ground, were places where it was dangerous to harbour anger and sacrilegious to shed blood. Men being pursued as criminals sought refuge in churches; reconciliations and bargains were made there. They were also places where folk might relax safely and indulge in joyful activities under the protection of God and the patron saints. "Bride-ales" or marriage-feasts were held in churchyards; and so were church ales, when ale brewed by the churchwardens was sold to boost parish funds. The moralising Robert Manning, in his tract *Handlyng Synne* (1303), hoped to curtail such goings-on during service time:

> Carols, wrestlings or summer games,
> Who so ever haunteth any such shames
> In church, other in churchyard,
> Of sacrilege he may be afeared;
> Or interludes, or singing,
> Or tabor beat, or other piping,
> All such thing forbidden is,
> While the priest standeth at mass

The association of holidays as well as sacred places with amusement was close: communities had traditional ways of celebrating them. During the Twelve Days of Christmas, for instance, it was usual to have dances and songs, and to entertain and be entertained by mime shows (or "mummings"). A proclamation of 1541 describes customs on the Feast of the Holy Innocents (December the twenty-eighth): "children being strangely decked out and apparelled to counterfeit priests, bishops and women, and so to be led with songs and dances from house to house blessing the people and gathering money and preaching in the pulpit". On May Day young folk went to the woods all night and returned with hawthorn-boughs and the maypole: and on Midsummer Eve they lit bonfires and jumped over them.

The medieval calendar was punctuated by holidays, such as Christmas, Shrove Tuesday, Easter, Midsummer or the Nativity of St John (June the twenty-fourth), and Michaelmas (September the twenty-ninth). The extent to which these were observed varied according to the custom of the borough or manor; and there were also locally observed holidays, varying with regional saints' cults. Dr Barbara Harvey has noted that in the early fourteenth century at Bourton-on-the-Hill (Gloucestershire) the Abbot of Westminster recognised at least thirty-nine days of every year as complete holidays if they fell on weekdays, plus extended holidays of four days each at Easter and Whitsun.

At such times ordinary routines and roles were suspended; and normal criteria of time and space were in abeyance. The rules of hierarchy might be suspended or turned topsy-turvy, the young lording it over the mature, servants pretending to be master, women belabouring men. The sense that the Twelve Days of Christmas are out of ordinary time, with a magic quality of other-worldliness, is well conveyed in the poem *Sir Gawain and the Green Knight.* Yet holiday games and licence also had important social functions. They re-affirmed cohesiveness and ritualised conflict. They licenced disrespect and debauchery; such licence reinforced norms. In a society where most people spied on their neighbours and denounced their peers' and inferiors' erratic behaviour, where there was little privacy or encouragement of individuality, the holiday was a safety-valve.

Mass assumed special importance to villagers on holidays, for then – often at a significant point in the agrarian year – the parochial community came together to seek the intercession of the saints for God's blessing on seed, crops, or livestock. Besides attendance at holiday Masses, parishioners were bound by canon law and provincial and diocesan decrees to fulfil many ecclesiastical obligations, which a variety of Church courts attempted to enforce, besides generally punishing sinfulness. They had to attend Sunday Mass in the parish church, make confession to its priest at least once a year and take communion from him at least three times. They were to receive from him baptism, the marriage blessing, and "extreme unction" before death, and were to be buried in the churchyard. Offerings and payments were owed to the priest for these services; and tithes were due to the rector from all their produce. Some obligations entailed parochial co-operation – for example the maintenance of the fabric of the nave of the church and the provision of the furniture and necessities of worship – and parish churchwardens were appointed to safeguard the fabric fund and the church treasures.

The parish thus imposed common obligations and entailed communal organisation: it was a force binding people together as a community.

MONMOUTH Gwent
OS 162 SO 510130

Monmouth is twenty miles south of Hereford (via the A456) and some forty miles north of Bristol, via the M4, historic Chepstow, and the A466 up the beautiful Wye valley. Its surrounding countryside is exceptionally attractive and full of interest: to the east are Offa's Dyke and the Forest of Dean; the south, Tintern and Chepstow; and to the west and north-west Raglan, Skenfrith, Grosmont and White castles.

Monmouth lies between the rivers Wye and Monnow at their confluence. In the years 1067–71 William the Conqueror's Norman follower William Fitz Osbern overran this part of the Welsh principality of Gwent, and established a castle here to guard against Welsh raids from the hilly region to the west. A borough was established for Norman settlers, but Fitz Osbern's son Roger forfeited his lands in 1075, and from the late eleventh until after the mid-thirteenth century the lordship was held by the Fitz Baderon family (also known as "de Monmouth"). Subsequently Henry III's grant of it to his son Edmund "Crouchback", Earl of Lancaster, brought it to the House of Lancaster. In 1404 Owain Glyn Dŵr's Welsh rebels pursued an English force to the gates of Monmouth. The castle was eventually dismantled after a siege by Parliamentary forces in 1646.

The castle was erected on a cliff by the banks of the Monnow, with the borough stretching down from it to the Wye. There is little left of its stone fortifications – principally fragments of the twelfth-century keep (of two storeys) and the adjacent great hall, possibly built by Edmund Crouchback: here the courts of the Marcher lordship of Monmouth were held. Edward III's son John of Gaunt, Duke of Lancaster, gave the castle to his own son Henry of Bolingbroke (the future Henry IV). In 1382, when Henry was sixteen, and his wife Mary thirteen, she gave birth to a child who died: but in 1386 they set up

house again at Monmouth, and in 1387 Mary bore another son there, the future Henry V. After bearing many more children, Mary died in childbirth in 1394, aged only twenty-five.

In the castle courtyard is Great Castle House (finished in 1673), built as a residence by Henry Somerset, Marquess of Worcester. The one remaining part of the town defences is the gate tower on Monnow Bridge at the end of Monnow Street: it was built in the thirteenth century to guard against Welsh attacks from the west, and has three over-hanging "machicoulis" through which missiles could be dropped on anyone assaulting the gate, from the chamber over it. This gate tower is a rare survival in England and Wales.

The parish church of St Mary incorporates parts of a twelfth century church of the priory founded in the late eleventh century, a cell of St Florent de Saumur. This was a Breton monastery: the family that ruled Monmouth in the late eleventh century had Breton origins, and Geoffrey of Monmouth (d.1155?), probably a monk here, was also of Breton descent. Geoffrey's *History of the Kings of Britain*, though almost entirely fictional, had a lasting influence on the imagination of the English and Welsh-speaking peoples: for he established the legendary history of King Arthur and of a previous line of mythical ancient British kings; and from his history Shakespeare derived the plots of *Cymbeline* and *King Lear*.

MUCHELNEY ABBEY and PRIEST'S HOUSE Somerset
OS 193 ST 428248

Muchelney, surrounded by the marshlands of Sedgemoor, is some twelve miles east of Taunton and exit 25 of the M5, via the A358, A378 and a minor road turning south in Langport. The abbey remains are in the village, and the Priest's House just to the north (at 429251): both are open from April until September. There are a number of very fine churches in this area, notably at Huish Episcopi (just to the north) and South Petherton (five miles south).

Here is an example of a priest's house dating from either the fourteenth or the fifteenth century (compare *Alfriston* and *Corbridge*). It is divided into three parts: there is a central hall open to the roof with, at one end, a ground floor parlour and an upstairs solar for the use of the priest; and at the other end, the service rooms. The priest was appointed by the abbot and convent of Muchelney to serve the parish church which stands next to the abbey. This was a Benedictine community founded in the eighth century – when Muchelney was doubtless a desolate spot in the midst of moorlands and marshes. Excavation has revealed an early eighth century monastic church which was incorporated as the crypt under the choir of a twelfth century church: though nothing remains standing either of this reconstruction or of the later parts of the medieval church. There are, however, remains of some of the monastic buildings on the south side of the cloister: and adjoining these is the well-preserved abbot's lodging, dating from the early sixteenth century.

Separate abbot's and prior's houses of this kind were being built with some style and sophistication from the fourteenth century onwards. As a justification for such relaxations of the austerities of monastic Rules, (which laid down that abbots must sleep in the same dormitory as their monks) abbots and priors may have argued that they ought to appear dignified for the honour of their house, and that it served the house's interest for them to entertain the nobility fittingly. The fourteenth century Abbot Cloune of Leicester, for instance, kept a pack of hounds to entertain the mightiest in the land – but it was noted that he also had a personal zeal for the sport. Though Muchelney was not a rich house, expense was not spared to fit the abbot's house out luxuriously. His parlour on the first floor is large, containing a fireplace with magnificently carved mantel, large windows and panelled wooden benches. Thus, while the abbot aspired to live like a lord, the local parish priest was housed like a well-to-do peasant.

See **Alfriston, Corbridge.**

The parish church of St Bartholomew is a good example of one rebuilt in a pretentious way in the thirteenth and fourteenth centuries: the earliest parts are the nave bays of c.1230–40, with delicately carved capitals. The church is best known, however, for its notable medieval tomb effigies, the most beautiful being that of Blanche Mortimer (d.1347), wife of Sir Peter de Grandison. She was born into one of the richest and most powerful families of the neighbouring Marches of Wales. Her father, Roger Mortimer, first earl of March, had been the lover of Edward II's queen Isabella, and procured the king's downfall and death: but Earl Roger was in turn overthrown and was executed in 1330. The man his daughter Blanche married, Sir Peter de Grandison, had also in his youth been involved in rebellion against Edward II, but was thereafter more careful. Blanche's effigy shows courtly good taste: her features, arms and hands are sensitively carved.

By contrast, the effigy of Walter Helyon, who died in 1375, also apparently an attempted likeness, portrays someone of much lower rank, a local squire or gentleman.

Helyon's effigy is unusual: it is of wood, and is remarkable in displaying everyday costume. It has been repainted, giving a good impression of its original appearance. Helyon is heavily but neatly bearded: his overtunic is fastened by a set of little decorative buttons; his knife and purse hang from his belt. There was concern in this period that social climbers were upsetting notions of rank by living too luxuriously, and in 1363 a statute was passed regulating the quality of clothes men ought to wear. Helyon, however, apparently did not aspire above his station. He was proud to have himself represented as a respectable freeman, not in armour like a knight, though the little lion at his feet perhaps hints that his courage was equal to a knight's. He has been compared in appearance to the Franklin in Chaucer's *Canterbury Tales*: such men were the precursors of the gentry and the backbone of shire society.

There are other fine effigies in the church – a knight and lady of c.1415, and Sir John Kyrle, who died in 1650. It is a rewarding place for students of the history of costume to visit.

MUCH MARCLE CHURCH
Herefordshire
OS 149 SO 657328
Much Marcle is five miles south-west of Ledbury by the A449 and about fifteen miles south-east of Hereford via the A438, the A4172 at Trumpet, and the A449 south. The church is in the centre of the village, and to its north-east is the charming small manor house of Hellens, once the home of Walter Helyon (open Wednesday, Saturday and Sunday afternoons in summer): Much Marcle is also famous for its local cider.

The painted wooden effigy of Walter Helyon was restored by The London Museum for the Chaucer Exhibition it staged in Kensington Palace fifteen years ago.

Neidpath Castle is picturesquely situated on a steep rise beside the river Tweed. It consists of an L-shaped tower-house and adjoining bailey: dating from the fourteenth century, the tower is an unusually early and intact survival of this form of fortification in lowland Scotland. It was the residence of a knightly family, the Hays, built by them on an impressive scale soon after they acquired the property in about 1310. They held the castle until 1686: their crest is on the outer gateway of the bailey, put there in the seventeenth century, when major alterations were made to the interior of the tower. Today the castle is owned by the Earl of Wemyss, a descendent

of the Duke of Queensberry who acquired it in 1686. From the later eighteenth century onwards it was let to tenants.

The tower-house is now uninhabited, but has been restored. Among its medieval features are a well sunk into the rock, mural chambers in the outer walls (these walls are from ten to twelve feet thick) and a particularly unpleasant pit dungeon. The great hall, most of whose features are post-medieval, is on the first floor: and on the second floor is the panelled "Queen Mary's Room", where Mary Queen of Scots is said to have slept in 1563, and her son James VI in 1587. Neidpath saw considerable fighting in the Civil

NEIDPATH CASTLE
Peebles, Borders
OS 73 NT 237405
The castle is superbly sited near the A72 about a mile west of Peebles, which is itself twenty-five miles south of Edinburgh via the A702 and A703: the castle is open from Easter until October. The primly attractive burgh of Peebles is surrounded by fine wooded countryside, and seven miles to the east (reached by turning south off the A72 at Innerleithen) is Traquair House, which claims to be the oldest inhabited home in Scotland (open Easter to October).

Wars: it was besieged by the Marquess of Montrose for Charles I in 1645, and by Cromwell's forces in 1650.

Nearby Peebles was a royal burgh in the Middle Ages, and suffered from English raids after the Scottish Wars of Independence. In 1406, for instance, an English force commanded by Sir Robert Umfraville burnt the town on market day; apparently it was then a centre of cloth distribution and perhaps production. The men of Northumberland gleefully nicknamed Umfraville "Robin Mendmarket". As late as the 1570s the burgesses believed that a stone wall round the town was a worthwhile new investment – possibly as much to protect them from the Scottish thieves of Liddesdale as from English invaders. The present main street, on high ground parallel to the Tweed, has features characteristic of urban settlement in medieval Scotland. The rows of houses are broken by "wynds" – narrow passages which led to cultivated strips, and which could be barricaded when watchmen on the dykes at the far ends of the fields signalled danger.

NUNNEY CASTLE Somerset
OS 183 ST 737457
Nunney is three and a half miles south-west of Frome, just off the A361 and some five miles west of Longleat, the Marquis of Bath's famous stately home. The castle is accessible throughout the year, and Nunney's parish chuch is also worth a visit: it contains an effigy which may well represent the castle-building Sir John.

Begun in 1373, Nunney Castle has been described as "an old soldier's dream", and tradition holds that its builder Sir John de la Mare paid for it with the spoils of his service in Edward III's French wars. Certainly its design – a tall rectangular block, with four round corner towers, which almost touch each other on the shorter faces of the rectangle – is more French than English, and may well have imitated that of strongholds Sir John had admired during his profitable military career. Living so far from the threat of foreign invasion, it was perhaps not strictly necessary for him to build such a heavily fortified residence, surrounded by a moat and topped with machicolations to support an overhanging gallery from which missiles could be dropped on attackers' heads: and it is thus not improbable that the old warrior was as much concerned to show off his wealth as with defence. Not until the Civil War of the 1640s, indeed, did the castle have to face an assault, and then Parliamentarian cannon made short work of it, causing the damage which eventually brought down its north wall.

OXFORD Oxfordshire
OS 164 SP 515065
The famous university city is fifty-seven miles north-west of London via the M40. Merton College (generally open to the public) is in Merton Street, which is off the east end of the High Street, near Magdalen Bridge. Returning to the High via Magpie Lane, the traveller emerges opposite the University Church of St Mary, and turns right towards Queen's Lane, which passes St Peters-in-the-East and leads to New College. Retracing his steps again to the High and now turning right, the traveller will eventually reach the crossroads called Carfax: here he has the choice of turning right to the churches of St Michael-at-the-Northgate (with its Saxon tower), St Mary Magdalen and St Giles: or left down St Aldates to Christ Church College, through which he must pass to reach the cathedral. Visitors should also see the splendid Ashmolean Museum in Beaumont Street.

Most of Oxford University's college buildings date from the late fourteenth century onwards. The earliest surviving are in Merton College, founded by Walter de Merton, who had a successful career in Henry III's employ. He was one of a type of clerical careerists who flourished with the expansion of royal central administration and its document-keeping in the thirteenth century: royal chancellor from 1261 until 1263, he was rewarded with the minor bishopric of Rochester. He used his profits of office to provide endowments for a number of scholars to live together and study for higher degrees (compare Robert Burnell's use of his profits at *Acton Burnell*). The college's first statute was approved in 1263–64.

The building of the present Merton college chapel was begun on a grand scale in about 1290. The choir was built first, the crossing in c.1330–35, the south transept in 1367–68 and the north transept in the early fifteenth century. The chapel is notable for its height, its fine proportions, and its geometrical window tracery; and for its surviving medieval stained glass, the earliest dating from the last decade of the thirteenth century. The college hall and the hall at the north-east corner of Front Quad are also basically thirteenth century buildings, while Mob Quad (1304–78) is Oxford's earliest surviving college quadrangle, with its earliest college library. Some of these buildings would still be recognisable to Merton's most famous medieval scholar – John Wycliffe (d.1384), who became a junior fellow in 1356: the English "father of heresies" and precursor of Protestantism, Wycliffe more than anyone else broke the intellectual mould of the medieval Church.

The origins of the medieval university can be traced to the twelfth century scholars who congregated and attracted pupils in this flourishing town, perhaps as famous then for its shoe and bootmaking as for its intellectual achievements. The university was to remain poorly endowed compared with its colleges: it had few buildings of its own. Some of the early ones remain, attached to the parish church of St Mary (the university church) in the High Street – a focal point of Oxford's skyline, with its soaring tower (late thirteenth century) and spire (early fourteenth century). On the north side of the church is the Congregation House, where the university's governing body met, and above this is the earliest library building, both dating from the early fourteenth century.

Walter de Merton and others after him were able to buy land in the centre of Oxford for colleges because the town's prosperity was declining; its weaving industry was in trouble by the last quarter of the thirteenth century, and the university thereafter became Oxford's main business. Its earlier prosperity had owed something to (and been reflected in) the number of religious houses there and in the vicinity. Their remains are fragmentary, except for St Frideswide's Priory, tucked away near a corner of Christ Church College's Tom Quad, and somewhat obscured by the college's impressive later buildings. The priory was an Augustinian house founded in honour of a female Anglo-Saxon saint by Henry I, who had a house just outside the town (whose site was near Beaumont Street) and a hunting-lodge not far off at Woodstock (whose site is in the grounds of Blenheim Palace). In 1525 Henry VIII's minister Cardinal Wolsey procured the dissolution of the priory and used its site and revenues for his new Cardinal College, unfinished when he fell from power. The college was taken under royal patronage as Christ Church, and the priory church (which Wolsey had intended to demolish) became in 1542 the cathedral of the new diocese of Oxford.

The building of St Frideswide's may have been started in the 1170s and continued into the early thirteenth century. Its present shape is box-like and rather small: it has lost part of its nave and was heavily restored in the nineteenth century. The Romanesque arches of the choir awkwardly vault across the triforium gallery: the fine pendant vault itself dates from the end of the fifteenth century. There is sensitively sculpted early thirteenth century arcading in the church and chapter-house: and at the east end of the cathedral the Lady Chapel and Latin Chapel date from the thirteenth and fourteenth centuries. Medieval glass survives in the Latin Chapel and St Lucy's Chapel and the church is rich in funeral monuments: its spire dates from the thirteenth century and part of the monastic cloister (rebuilt at the end of the fifteenth century) survives.

The parish churches of St Peter-in-the-East (Queen's Lane) and St Giles (St Giles Street) have thirteenth century features; while St Mary Magdalen (Magdalen Street and St Giles Street) has a south aisle dated c.1330. There are also remaining sections of the new set of town walls built 1226–40, the best preserved section (with tall semi-circular towers) being visible in New College Garden. *See* **Acton Burnell.**

Set in beautiful countryside and in a delightful small town famous for its profusion of timbered 'black and white' houses, the essentially fourteenth century church of St Mary at Pembridge contains four fine medieval tomb-effigies – a gowned lawyer and his wife of c.1320 and a behatted country gentleman of c.1370, also with his lady. Its most remarkable feature, however, is its unusual detached "bell-house", an octagonal stone building with a triple-pyramid wooden roof: within is a masterpiece of medieval carpentry, a great bell frame of mighty timbers reinforced by a complex and ingenious system of cross-bracing.

PEMBRIDGE Herefordshire
OS 149 SO 391580
Pembridge is seven miles west of Leominster ("lemster"), on the A44 to Kington: the church is set back from the road, off the little market place with its timbered Market House and handsome timbered New Inn.

Pembroke castle was founded in 1090, when the Norman Arnulf of Montgomery sailed into Milford Haven and dug in on the tip of the promontory jutting into the bay between the Pembroke river and the stream known as Monkton Pill. One of the features which attracted the Normans to fortify this headland was the Wogan, a dry cavern seventy feet long and forty feet broad on the north side, into which supplies could be loaded from boats. It was reached by stairs from the ruined hall adjacent to the curtain wall of the inner bailey. This bailey, covering the end of the promontory, was the nucleus of Arnulf's base: the origin and head of what was to become the powerful Earldom of Pembroke. The stone curtain walls which surround the roughly triangular area date from the twelfth and early thirteenth centuries, and the landward wall, leading to the outer bailey, had two semi-circular towers among its defences, but was dominated by the great round keep in the inner bailey, still an awesome landmark in the haven. The keep, of five storeys, is eighty feet high, with walls averaging fifteen feet in thickness: entrance was by drawbridge to the first floor. Roofing the top storey is a stone dome, which had a parapet walk of its own in addition to the one round the top of the keep's walls, confronting assailants with two rings of concentrated fire.

The outer bailey, stretching inland, is much bigger. Its curtain wall, towers and gatehouse are thirteenth century; and the gatehouse, fronted by semi-circular towers, and projecting deeply from the curtain wall at the front and back, bears comparison with those built as strongpoints in Edward I's Welsh castles. It had a barbican: the gateway passage is protected by two portcullises and three "murder holes", and if any besiegers nevertheless managed to burst into the bailey, the garrison could rain shot on the backs of their necks from the parapet between the two round towers on the rear of the gatehouse.

The earldom and castle were acquired by marriage in 1189 by William the Marshal; after the failure of the Marshal line Henry III granted them to his half-brother Aymer de Valence, and for much of the fourteenth century they were in the Hastings family. The future Henry VII was born in the castle in 1457: his mother, Margaret Beaufort, Countess of Richmond, was then aged thirteen; his uncle Jasper Tudor was Earl of Pembroke. The castle briefly saw action in the Wars of the Roses, as a result of Jasper's adherence to the losing Lancastrian side – Henry VI was his half-brother. In 1461 a Lancastrian garrison surrendered to Edward IV's partisan Lord Herbert (who was to receive the earldom and castle from him); and in 1471, in the aftermath of the Lancastrian defeat at *Tewkesbury*, Jasper fortified himself with his

PEMBROKE CASTLE Dyfed
OS 158 SN 982017
Pembroke is near the south-western tip of Wales, some forty-five miles west of Swansea via the M4, A48 to Carmarthen, A40 and A477: the fine castle is open daily, except on winter Sundays. Two miles east of Pembroke (via the A4139) is Lamphey, with its Bishop's Palace: and further east on the same road are Manorbier Castle and historic Tenby.

young nephew Henry in Pembroke Castle. He was besieged by the Yorkist Morgan Thomas "and kept in with ditch and trench that he might not escape", but a rescue was effected by Welsh Lancastrians. Nevertheless, Jasper and Henry had to flee abroad from Tenby, to return fourteen years later, landing in Milford Haven and riding to confront Richard III at Bosworth.

The castle housed a Parliamentary garrison in the Civil War, but in 1648 it was held with the town, whose walls connected with those of the castle's outer bailey, against Cromwell. The defences were then seriously damaged by artillery bombardment and the subsequent deliberate destruction. Relics from the medieval borough founded by the Normans are the church of Monkton Priory and the parish churches of St Mary and St Michael.

See **Tewkesbury**.

PENSHURST PLACE Kent
OS 188 TQ 527440

The house is four miles south-west of Tonbridge (via the A21, A26 and B2176) and thus some thirty-five miles south-east of London: it is open from April until October. This part of Kent is almost unrivalled for stately homes: immediately to the west of Penshurst are Chiddingstone and Hever Castles, and within ten miles to the north are Knole (near Sevenoaks), Ightham Mote and Old Scoar Manor at Plaxtol.

John de Pulteney was a draper who was four times Lord Mayor of London between 1333 and 1337. Leading London merchants amassed great wealth as they gained control of an increasing share of England's export trade, and they were starting to express their wealth by living like lords rather than burgesses. Pulteney got himself knighted; he arranged to be buried in St Paul's Cathedral; he appointed its bishop and an earl to supervise the execution of his will. To the latter he bequeathed a ring set with two great diamonds, two enamelled silver flagons, a cup, a spoon and a matching salt cellar. But Pulteney dazzled with more than his tableware and his rings – he had another one set with a ruby which, he boasted, was "of great value and beauty" – for he also built Penshurst Place, a splendid country house fit for a baron. Its great hall has the original tiled floor, the raised dais where the more eminent guests dined, a central hearth with a louvre to let out the smoke, a roof of carved oak beams, and traceried windows. The screens date from after 1552, for they have the Ragged Staff badge adopted by Sir Henry Sidney, who had recently married into the Earl of Warwick's family, whose badge it was. Behind the screens three doorways led to the kitchen, buttery and pantry: the kitchen, however, no longer exists.

Adjoining Pulteney's house is the Buckingham Building, a hall over an undercroft whose original features have been considerably altered. The finials of its gables are carved as falcons and ibex, badges of John Duke of Bedford (d.1436), its probable builder. He bought Penshurst in 1430, and it was conveniently placed for him to reach Westminster or northern France, where this stern, able brother of Henry V strove – as Regent of France for his little nephew Henry VI – to uphold English rule. It was he who had to deal with the challenge of St Joan of Arc. Considerable additions were also made to Penshurst Place in the Elizabethan period and the early seventeenth century. It was there that Sir Henry Sidney's son Philip was born in 1554: the epitome of the Elizabethan courtier-poet and author of *Arcadia*, Philip Sidney died nobly in the Queen's wars in 1586.

The village has a pleasant atmosphere. The parish church was heavily restored in the nineteenth century, but has interior features dating from the fourteenth and fifteenth centuries (for instance the nave arcades). Within is the marble tomb-effigy of Sir Stephen de Penchester (d.1299), in chain-mail, and in the Sidney Chapel is the tomb of Sir William Sidney (d.1553). He had been steward of the sickly young Edward VI's household, and was rewarded for his services by a royal grant of Penshurst Place.

PETERBOROUGH
Cambridgeshire
OS 142 TL 195986

Peterborough is some eighty miles north of London, via the A1: and the cathedral is near the centre of the largely modern and rather unattractive city. There is much of interest in the flat surrounding countryside, including Longthorpe Tower immediately to the west, near the A47; and Crowland and Thorney abbeys to the north.

Peterborough was one of the monasteries founded during the expansion of monasticism in Anglo-Saxon England, by the royal house of the kingdom of Mercia. The invading Danes sacked it in about 870, but it was refounded in 972 by the monastic reformer Bishop Aethelwold of Winchester under the patronage of King Edgar: this was part of the extension of the Wessex monarchy's power over England. The abbey was richly endowed with estates; and over many of the adjacent lands it exercised judicial rights usually pertaining to the king's officials. This "soke" (or liberty) of Peterborough, formed a separate county, and included the town growing up at the abbey's gates – which only acquired a mayor in 1874, after its great expansion during the Industrial Revolution. The jurisdiction and tenurial policies of the monks were not always congenial to their tenants: and during the Peasants' Revolt of 1381 some of the people of the soke plotted to kill the abbot, but failed to carry out their purpose.

The Normans had at first found it difficult to control the abbey and soke, largely because of the guerilla activities of an Anglo-Saxon resistance leader who lurked in the neighbouring Fenlands, Hereward the Wake – whose exploits were embroidered by the Victorian writer Charles Kingsley. In 1070 Hereward sacked the monastery, but spared the church. Despite control by Norman abbots, Peterborough for long remained a centre of Anglo-Saxon culture and sentiment; its monks kept up the writing of annals in the English language, in a version of the Anglo-Saxon Chronicle, till as late as 1154.

In 1116 the church was burnt down, and

A part of the exquisitely decorated ceiling in Peterborough Cathedral.

Abbot John de Seez initiated the building of a new one, in which services were being held in 1143; the nave was completed by 1194. This church substantially remains, one of the most complete and finest examples of a great Romanesque church in Britain. But it is most famous for its dramatic west front (*c.*1180–1238), a "portico" or porch extended in front of the Romanesque west wall. The portico has a high vaulted roof and a front formed by three massive, deeply recessed pointed arches, eighty-one feet high. These are offset by narrow corner towers with spires (which complement the central tower), and by matching overhead gables. A fifteenth century porch with a chamber above it project under the central arch.

The nave has a rare early medieval wooden ceiling (*c.*1220–38), painted in a lozenge pattern with saints, kings and queens, monsters, a Janus head, and a monkey on a goat. In the south presbytery aisle are the tombs of four abbots (*c.*1195–*c.*1225), with early examples of marble effigies. The monastic church survived the Dissolution intact because in 1541 it became the cathedral of the new diocese of Peterborough, and in the sixteenth century it was the burial place of two tragic queens. Henry VIII's discarded first wife, Catherine of Aragon, is buried in the north choir aisle: and the corpse of Mary Queen of Scots was interred here (in the south choir aisle) after her execution at Fotheringhay Castle in 1587, but her son James I had it removed to Westminster Abbey in 1612. In the west transept, over his burial-place, is a portrait of the local grave-digger, Old Scarlett, who died in 1594 aged ninety-eight. He has a spade, pickaxe, keys, and a whip for driving dogs out of the Cathedral; at his feet is a skull: an inscription reflects on his trade and his mortality:

Hee had inter'd two queenes within this place
And this townes householders in his lives space
Twice over: but at length his owne turne came.
What hee for others did for him the same
Was done.

In the Minster Yard there are fragmentary remains of the monastic buildings, some of them incorporated into later structures: there are also gateways and parts of the infirmary and cloisters. In the city is the church of St John the Baptist, dating from the fifteenth century, and the Guild Hall in Market Place (1671), which had a butter market under its open arches.

The vault above the central crossing.

PLUSCARDEN PRIORY
Grampian
OS 28 NJ 142577
Once again flourishing and occupied by monks, the priory is in the north of Scotland, some thirty-five miles east of Inverness and six miles south-west of Elgin, via the B9010 and a minor road turning west at Pittendreich. Visitors are most welcome at any reasonable time.

The impulse to refine still further the austerities of the monastic life had not died out by the end of the twelfth century, though alternative (and, to the traditionalist, sometimes alarming) models of the righteous life were coming into fashion on the continent. Viard was a monk of the austere Carthusian Order at Lugny in Burgundy, who obtained his abbot's permission to live as a hermit in a cave in the Val des Choux ("Cabbage Valley", in Latin Vallis Caulium). Duke Odo of Burgundy, impressed by Viard and about to set out on crusade, vowed that if he returned safely he would found a new Order with Viard at its head. This he accomplished.

The Valliscaulian Order was one of extreme austerity. Only three houses were founded in Scotland, all in 1230 – Ardchattan (Argyll), Beauly (Inverness-shire) and Pluscarden. Their foundation shows how in touch Scottish noble society was with current

monastic trends in France – though the new movements of the friars (in Scotland as elsewhere) evoked more enthusiasm from recruits and patrons. The monks at Pluscarden do not seem to have been ever able to afford to build the nave of their church, but the thirteenth century choir, transepts and crossing remain, built on an impressive scale: so do some of the monastic buildings, though these were heavily restored in the nineteenth and twentieth centuries.

In the event, the priory faltered in the fifteenth century: since the number of monks had fallen to six, it was handed over to the Benedictines in 1453–54. But what makes Pluscarden special in Britain is that it is a medieval monastery to which monks have returned. In 1948 six Benedictines came there from Prinknash Abbey (Gloucestershire), and they have restored the abbey and its ancient way of life.

RHUDDLAN CASTLE Clwyd
OS 116 SJ 025778
Rhuddlan is near the north-east coast of Wales, three miles south of Rhyl on the A547: just to the south is the little cathedral city of St Asaph, and some fourteen miles to the east (via Holywell with its healing springs) is Flint Castle.

The first motte-and-bailey castle was set up here, on the orders of William the Conqueror, by the Norman Robert of Rhuddlan, deputy of Hugh Earl of Chester. A borough was also established, and traces of its defensive earthworks survive. Rhuddlan changed hands a number of times in the twelfth and thirteenth centuries in frontier fighting between the Welsh and Anglo-Normans. In 1277 Edward I stopped here during his first campaign against Llywelyn Prince of Wales, and decided to found a new castle and borough to the north of the earlier site. The castle, of which James of St George was architect, was constructed between 1272 to 1282 on high ground overlooking the river Clwyd. It was planned (characteristically of this architect) as two concentric lines of fortification. The lower walls of the outer line have been almost entirely destroyed, but at the

south-west corner was a dock gate, protected by the high Gillot's Tower projecting outwards from the wall. The intention was to enable ships to supply the castle from the Clwyd, which was canalised to facilitate access from the sea – often an important consideration in the siting and design of Edwardian castles.

The defences of the inner bailey are better preserved. It is designed as a square set at an angle, with twin-towered gatehouses at the east and west corners and single towers projecting from the north and south angles. The principal residential apartments were in the towers and courtyard buildings of this inner ward and a few traces of them survive. It was in this castle that Edward I issued the Statute of Rhuddlan (1284), setting up his new system of government in North Wales.

Scarred drum towers flank the western gatehouse at Rhuddlan.

Rievaulx was the first Cistercian house in the north of England, founded as a result of a mission sent from Clairvaux by St Bernard in 1131. Walter Espec, lord of Helmsley (remains of whose castle still stand) granted lands to William, the first abbot, and his twelve monks, including the site of the monastery on the bank of the river Rye. One of the early monks, Walter Daniel, has left a description of the setting which shows an intense appreciation of the countryside:

"High hills surround the valley, encircling it like a crown. These are clothed by trees of various sorts and maintain in pleasant retreats the privacy of the vale, providing for the monks a kind of second paradise of wooded delight. From the loftiest rocks the waters wind and tumble down to the valley below; and as they make their hasty way through the lesser passages and narrower beds and spread themselves in wider rills, they give out a gentle murmur of soft sound and join together in the sweet notes of a delicious melody."

Rievaulx was for a time the most influential Cistercian house in Britain, sending out monks to form daughter-houses. Under the devout and paternalistic rule of Ailred (d.1167), whose life Walter Daniel wrote, it grew into a large community, with 140 monks and at least 500 of the lay brethren (*conversi*) which were a feature of the Order in its early phase.

The nave of the church dates from c.1135–40; it is of nine bays, with aisles, and is severe in style, admirably reflecting the intensity of the early Cistercians' ideals. The church extended only two bays east of the

RIEVAULX ABBEY
North Yorkshire
OS 100 SE 577849
Rievaulx is beautifully set in a wooded valley two miles west of Helmsley (which is twenty miles north of York via the B1363). Helmsley itself is worth a visit for its fine castle (611836) and from there the traveller can reach Rievaulx either by a delightful riverside walk or (by car) via the B1257 west and a signposted minor road. Not far to the south-west (via the A170) is Byland Abbey, another impressive ruin, and Newburgh Priory, a stately home.

tower, but in about 1230 the eastern end was rebuilt and enlarged on a grandiose scale. A choir and presbytery extending to seven bays was built; the style was now more decorative. At the end of the twelfth century a reconstruction of the conventual buildings was undertaken, and during the fourteenth century they were adapted (as was the church) to cope with the disappearance of the *conversi*, who had been separately housed and had their own choir. At the dissolution of the monastery in 1538 there were only twenty-two monks there.

The ruins of Rievaulx Abbey.

RIPON North Yorkshire
OS 99 SE 314713

The small but attractive city of Ripon is about twenty-five miles north-west of York, via the A59 and B6265 through Boroughbridge: it can also easily be reached from the A1, which runs just to the east of it. Centred on its fine market square (where the Wakeman blows his horn nightly) Ripon makes an ideal centre for touring this interesting part of Yorkshire: signposted immediately to the west are the impressive ruins of Fountains Abbey; to the south (via the A61) are Ripley and Knaresborough castles; and to the north-west are the beautiful Yorkshire Dales.

A monastery was founded here in the mid-seventh century by that fiery Northumbrian bishop Wilfrid. Miraculously, as at Hexham, the crypt of his church survives, despite the destruction of the monastery by the Danes. In the north wall of this crypt is a narrow hole, nicknamed Wilfrid's Needle. Ability to crawl through this was regarded as a proof of chastity – a custom which was a variation on the early medieval judicial process of proving innocence by undergoing an ordeal.

After the Norman Conquest the church was served by secular canons, and was under the patronage of the Archbishops of York, whose manor Ripon was – they had a country house here. In the time of Thomas of Bayeux, the first Norman archbishop, a new church was built, of which the vaulted undercroft and the chapel at the east end of the chapterhouse survive. In the archiepiscopate of Roger Pont l'Eveque (1154–81), there was a further rebuilding; two bays of its aisleless

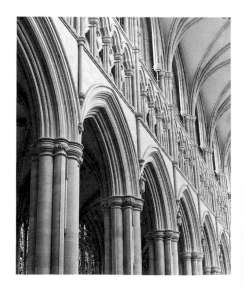

nave remain at the west end. Then, in the early thirteenth century, the west front was reconstructed; its low twin towers originally had lead-coated wooden spires: and subsequently Archbishop Romanus (1286–98) patronised the rebuilding of the eastern part of the choir, whose great east window has one of the finest surviving schemes of geometrical tracery. The choir roof bosses have carvings of Biblical scenes and ecclesiastical figures; the canopied choir stalls (c.1490) have an entertaining collection of misericord carvings. In the fourteenth century a Lady Chapel was built, unusually, over the chapter-house.

The Minster and people of Ripon have suffered many vicissitudes over the centuries. In Edward II's reign Ripon came within the reach of deep-penetrating Scottish raids, and in 1318 the inhabitants barricaded themselves for three days in the church, then paid a ransom to get rid of the Scots. The raiders, however, were back next year. The college of canons was dissolved in Edward VI's reign, in 1547, but re-established by James I in 1604. In 1643 parliamentary troops occupying the town went on an orgy of puritanical destruction in the church, smashing the stained glass windows, of which only a few fragments remain.

Near the Minster is the half-timbered "Wakeman's House", dating from the fourteenth century, which now houses a museum of local history. The Wakeman (watchman) was head of the town council; and as during the Middle Ages his hornblower still blows his horn when the Minster bell tolls the curfew at nine o'clock on every evening of the year. Anyone abroad after then was suspected of being up to no good.

See **Hexham.**

Left, early medieval work in the nave, and above, the choir of Ripon Minster.

A massive medieval column at the crossing in Ripon Minster.

ROTHESAY CASTLE
Island of Bute, Strathclyde
OS 63 NS 087647

Rothesay is the capital of the Island of Bute, which lies in the Firth of Clyde some thirty miles west of Glasgow. It is best reached from Glasgow via the M8, the A8, and the A78 to Wemyss Bay, whence a half hour trip on a car ferry carries the traveller directly to Rothesay.

By about 1200 the Stewarts (ancestors of the royal dynasty) had established themselves on the Isle of Bute in the Firth of Clyde, though the kings of Norway and the Hebridean lords also regarded the island as within their spheres of influence. To guard their precariously-held acquisition, the Stewarts built a castle near the shore on the Bay of Rothesay, and its stone curtain wall and moat surrounding a circular bailey survive. In 1230 the castle was besieged by Norsemen and islanders, who hacked at its walls with their axes and broke in, despite the burning pitch hurled down on them: they slew the keeper of the castle, probably one of the Stewarts. In 1263 Norwegians from a royal invasion fleet again took the castle. During the thirteenth century the four existing great round towers were added to the curtain wall, and in the early sixteenth century James IV and James V, intent on imposing their authority in the west, added the outworks in front of the gatehouse. The only domestic building standing is the chapel in the bailey.

The Outlaw and the Greenwood

In 1356 King John II of France was escorted to England as a prisoner, captured at the battle of Poitiers, a great triumph for the English Crown. He was accompanied by his captor, the Black Prince, who paid him elaborate courtesies. As they rode through Kent, they were ambushed near a forest by a company of over 500 men clad in green – robbers and outlaws who lived in the forest. The French king was alarmed, the prince was unperturbed; the robbers let them pass without harm.

The robbers behaved prudently. They may have flattered themselves that they were the king's loyal subjects, who would not insult the king's son or the king's exalted prisoner: perhaps their heroes were those famous loyal subjects, Robin Hood and his men. Groups like these Kentish robbers were a recurring phenomenon in medieval England: criminal bands who often lived rough and poached game, their highway robberies were an accustomed nuisance. The poet William Langland, writing at the end of our period, said "there are outlaws lurking in the woods and hiding under the banks, who can see every man that passes. They note carefully who goes in front and who follows behind, which men are on horseback and which on foot – for a man on horseback is bolder than one on foot". Highway robbery was hard to suppress, for there were no regular police forces, though adult male peasants were organised into groups known as "tithings" under a constable or "headborough". On the constables' orders (sometimes passed on from the sheriff) tithings pursued, arrested and detained suspected criminals.

The ballads of Robin Hood presented the robbers as kindly men who only attacked malevolent landowners and officials. Perhaps this was wishful thinking, an attempt to soften reality – and perhaps, too, it was an attempt to influence the behaviour of real robbers. Many of these may have been victims of the law and fugitives from harsh masters rather than hardened criminals, with whom the ballads' contrast between oppressive law and natural justice would have struck an answering note.

Was there really a person called Robin Hood who behaved in the way described in the ballads? The sources make it difficult to prove. The earliest reference to popular ballads circulating about Robin Hood occurs in about 1370, in William Langland's didactic English poem, *Piers the Ploughman*. Such ballads were recited by professional minstrels, who altered the story, the setting and the moral to suit their audience. Historical origins were therefore likely to become forgotten and obscured, and the first written Robin Hood ballad dates only from c.1500. Not surprisingly, the Robin of this ballad is very much a contemporary figure, and his apparel, diet, and courteous, devout behaviour are gentlemanly attributes. Called a "yeoman" (an ambiguous style), he seems like one of those rich later medieval peasants who were distancing themselves from their less well-off neighbours.

Professor Barrie Dobson and John Taylor have pointed out that in this version, Robin's activities were not fixed in Sherwood Forest (Nottinghamshire), but north of Doncaster (Yorkshire), in Barnsdale and along a precisely referenced stretch of the Great North Road (now the A1) long notorious for highway robberies. Could it be then, that there was a famous Yorkshire robber, perhaps in the thirteenth century, who operated in Barnsdale and whose name was Robin Hood?

RYE East Sussex
OS 189 TQ 920205

Impressively sited overlooking Romney Marsh, Rye is eleven miles north-east of Hastings via the A259, but can be most easily reached from London via the M20 to Ashford and the A2070 south. Immediately south is the ancient port of Winchelsea and (via footpaths) Henry VIII's Camber Castle: and to the east is New Romney and the lonely churches of the Marsh.

The Cinque Ports were a confederation of originally five (French, "cinque") Channel ports – Hastings in Sussex and Romney, Hythe, Dover and Sandwich in Kent. The confederation's origins go back before the Norman Conquest, and it grew in wealth and power in the twelfth and thirteenth centuries mainly through trade with Flanders, the principal commercial and industrial region of north-west Europe. The kings of England appreciated the naval and financial support to be milked from the Cinque Ports, granting them many privileges in return: from 1206 onwards, for instance, their leading burgesses were allowed to style themselves by the superior title of "baron". But some of the ports started to be cut off from the English Channel by silting, and they were vulnerable to French raids during the Hundred Years War (1337–1453). They were less able to weather the economic recession of the fourteenth and fifteenth centuries than some of their competitors, and as they declined London merchants picked up much of their trade.

Rye was admitted as a full member of the confederacy only in about 1336, but long before then it had been a prosperous port. This is reflected in the large scale of its parish church of St Mary and in the later alterations to it. The impressive Ypres Tower (named

after a tenant) dates mainly from the thirteenth century: it was built to guard the sea approaches at the north-west corner of the town; and is of three storeys with three-quarter-round towers at the corners.

Rye was built beside the river Rother, on a long hill which rises dramatically from what is now the surrounding plain. The street plan of its centre is still essentially that of the medieval town. In 1339 it was sacked by the French, and it may have been in response to this that stone walls and gates were built. The north-east gate (the Landgate) survives, its two lower storeys built in about 1340, its third one probaly repaired or added after 1377, when a combined force of French and Castilians sacked the town. Rye's trade suffered from silting-up: the sea is now about two miles away. There are also many worthwhile buildings dating from the sixteenth century and later, such as the Peacock School in the High Street (1636) and the George Hotel opposite (c.1719). The Mermaid Inn in Mermaid Street ((c.1500) has a thirteenth-century cellar: in the eighteenth century it was a great meeting-place for smugglers. The American novelist Henry James owned Lamb House (early eighteenth century) near the Mermaid Inn, and lived there until his death in 1916.

ST DAVIDS Dyfed
OS 157 SM 751254

The tiny cathedral city stands on the south-western tip of Wales, some sixty miles west of Swansea via the M4, A48 to Camarthen, A40 to Haverfordwest and A487. The rocky coastline hereabouts is outstandingly beautiful, and can be conveniently seen by walking stretches of the Pembrokeshire Coast Path, easily reached via minor roads west of St Davids: not far to the east is the wild country of the Preseli Hills.

St David founded a monastic settlement here in the sixth century; it became the seat of the senior Welsh bishopric but, like so many other religious communities, suffered as a result of Viking raids. In 1081 William the Conqueror paid a visit; and in the twelfth century, when St Davids was part of the Norman Earldom of *Pembroke*, the bishopric was revived. In the following century Prior John of Ewenny had revealed to him a vision the burial place of St David, outside the south door of the cathedral: excavation there revealed a body, which was solemnly installed in a shrine in the cathedral in 1275.

The discovery of St David's remains added to the prestige of the cathedral and bishopric; and with pilgrims came offerings and endowments. Edward I and his queen Eleanor visited the new shrine in 1284. In 1280 the bishopric had been granted to an Englishman, Thomas Bek (d.1293), and it was probably he who started building a new bishop's palace, commensurate as he saw it with the dignity of his office. The buildings form a quadrangular courtyard, partly made up by existing works: these new buildings, dating from the last twenty years of the thirteenth century, make up the present eastern range – gatehouse, chapel, solar and hall. A much grander hall was subsequently built along the south wall, probably the work of Bishop Gower (d.1347), and there was a general reconstruction of the domestic buildings shortly after Gower's death.

The ruins give a good impression of what

was probably one of the grandest bishop's palaces in medieval Britain. Bishop Gower's great hall, in particular, has startling, almost Moorish exterior decorations – a combination of corbelled-out parapets, extravagantly large and repetitive arcades and white and purple stonework.

The adjacent cathedral is staid by comparison. It is cruciform, with low aisles and an imposing central tower of three stages: most of the cathedral is a rebuilding prompted by the collapse of a previous tower in 1220, and perhaps further stimulated by St David's miraculous reappearance. Much of it dates from Bishop Gower's episcopate, as does the fine choir screen, and there are stalls with misericord carvings dating from the fifteenth century. A tomb with a fourteenth century knightly effigy is reputed to be that of the Lord Rhys ap Gruffydd (d.1197), who stemmed the tide of Norman advance in Wales, and here also is the tomb of Edmund Tudor, Earl of Richmond (d.1456), brought to St Davids from the Franciscan friary at Carmarthen. Edmund, Henry VI's half-brother, died in his early twenties: his most memorable act was to father the future Henry VII.

The boundary of the cathedral close is marked by a medieval wall: one of its gates, Porth y Twr (c.1300) remains. St Davids has a pleasant village-like atmosphere; at its centre is the restored medieval market cross of the borough, which was owned by the bishops.

See Pembroke

SALISBURY Wiltshire
OS 184 SU 140300

Salisbury is eighty-eight miles south-west of London via the M3 and A30. The beautiful Cathedral Close is to the south of the city centre, by the river Avon: and in the city itself (reached from the Close via the medieval North Gate) St Thomas's church in the High Street is especially worth a visit for its fine "Doom" wall-painting. Wilton House is two and a half miles to the west (open April–October); Old Sarum (138327) is immediately to the north, via the A345; and further north are the great prehistoric temples of Stonehenge (near Amesbury) and Avebury (west of Marlborough).

Salisbury Cathedral's spire, the third tallest in Europe.

In 1217 Bishop Richard Poore successfully petitioned the Pope for permission to rebuild his cathedral on a new site. He eventually chose one on low-lying ground by a bend of the river Avon, just over a mile away from the existing hill-top settlement of Old Sarum, where there was a royal castle, borough and cathedral – the latter built after the two sees of Sherborne and Ramsbury were united and transferred there in 1075. The excavated outlines of the Norman cathedral can be seen at Old Sarum, but the shrine of the bishop who completed the first Norman cathedral there, St Osmund (d.1099) is now in the nave of Salisbury Cathedral: it has openings for pilgrims to place their diseased limbs in. Towards the west end of the nave is the tomb effigy of Bishop Roger (d.1139), who rebuilt the cathedral at Old Sarum on a grander scale, and on the opposite side is an effigy which may have marked the heart burial of Bishop Poore.

93

The building of a cathedral on the new site began in 1220; the master mason was Nicholas of Ely, under the supervision of one of the canons, Elias of Dereham. Salisbury has the most unified design of any English medieval cathedral, and the style is set in the eastern Trinity or Lady Chapel, with its tall thin columns and narrow lancet windows, its simple crossover vaulting ribs and contrasting black Purbeck marble and limestone. In 1225 the bodies of three previous bishops, including Osmund, were transferred to this chapel. The elegant design was elaborated elsewhere, intensified by trefoiled heads to arches and quatrefoils in the clerestories. By 1258 the choir, transepts and nave were completed; and the richly sculpted west front was finished by 1265: during the early fourteenth century two stages were added to the central tower, and so was the spire, 404 feet high and now the third highest in Europe. The interior wooden scaffold and windlass used to build the spire still remain in position, but the foundations and piers at the crossing proved insufficient for its additional weight; so a new vault and buttresses were built, and in the fifteenth century two great stone girder arches were added.

Many of the medieval furnishings and tombs in the church have been destroyed or shifted around, but there is a medieval chest for storing vestments, still in use, in the south-east transept. Near the north door of the nave is a restored clock mechanism dating from 1386 or before, which was originally in a detached belfry. On the south side of the nave is the tomb and effigy of Henry II's illegitimate son William Longespée, Earl of Salisbury. The mailed figure (one of the earliest surviving knightly effigies in England) is vigorously carved, and covered by his great war shield. Nearby is a similar effigy of his son William – a genuine crusader effigy, for this William took part in the crusade led by the

Far left, a view of the cloisters, the earliest surviving and the largest attached to any English cathedral. Left, sculptures on the north buttress flanking the central doors in the west front. Above, the cathedral nave.

King of France, Louis IX (St Louis) and was killed at the battle of Mansurah (1250) in Egypt, in which the reckless advance of the French chivalry was a prelude to the disaster which overtook the crusading army. In the south-east transept is the canopied tomb of Bishop Giles of Bridport (d.1262): sculptures on the canopy depict his homage for the see, his consecration, his death and the carrying of his soul to heaven by an angel. In the cathedral there are also notable later medieval and early modern monuments.

The cloisters (c.1263–70) are the earliest surviving ones – and the largest – attached to any English cathedral. The octagonal chapter-house (c.1263–84) has a vault springing from a central pillar, and above the wall seats of the chapter are carvings of Old Testament scenes: among the treasures displayed there is one of the four surviving contemporary copies of Magna Carta. The Cathedral Close is perhaps the most beautiful, as well as the most spacious, in England. On two sides it is bounded by the river and on the other two by a wall with three gates: Edward III granted a licence for it to be enclosed by a defensive wall in 1327. The Close has a notable collection of medieval and later houses. To the south of the cathedral the Bishop's Palace (now the Cathedral School) has Bishop Poore's original hall.

The borough which the bishops founded to the north and east of the Close, whose streets still reflect the original grid pattern, is one of the conspicuous success stories among English medieval new towns. The town flourished as a natural market centre for a prosperous region: the building of Harnham Bridge over the Avon to the south of the Close attracted long-distance trade in wool, and Salisbury itself was to become a considerable cloth-producing centre. Among its medieval buildings are parts of the Hospital of St Nicholas near Harnham Bridge (an almshouse existing in the thirteenth century) and the churches of St Martin and St Thomas. The Poultry Cross dates from the fifteenth century.

SHERWOOD FOREST

Nottinghamshire
OS 120 SK 620680

The most extensive remains of the great "shire wood" lie between Worksop and Mansfield, in the area bounded by the A60 to the west and A614 to the east. At their hub is the Sherwood Forest Visitor Centre (SK 620680) immediately north of Edwinstowe, which is on the A6075 just east of Ollerton and some eight miles east of the main A1. Papplewick church (SK 546515) is in the grounds of the Hall to the north of the village, which is seven miles south of Mansfield via the A60 and B683: and Skegby church (SK 493610) is immediately west of Mansfield, near the B6014.

Sherwood Forest stretched northwards from near Nottingham towards Worksop, covering an area about twenty miles long and eight miles broad. The royal foresters there and the justices of the forest seem to have had mixed success in safeguarding the king's rights, for by the end of the twelfth century Sherwood was notorious as a haunt of robbers, who presumably lived off the king's deer. Today 450 acres of ancient oak woodland are preserved as Sherwood Forest Country Park. Near Edwinstowe (in whose parish church Robin Hood is alleged to have been married), the Sherwood Forest Visitor Centre provides an introduction to the forest and an exhibition about Robin Hood. In fact, the famous outlaw's association with the forest occurs only in later, post-medieval ballads: and as Professor Holt has pointed out, the associations of particular places in the forest with him and his followers can nearly all be dated only as far back as the nineteenth century. In the parish church of St Andrew, Skegby, near Mansfield, there is a monument of c.1300 to one of the forest's officials, displaying his horn: and in St James's, Papplewick, there are monuments of two forest officials, one with his sling, bow and arrows, the other with a knife.

The Weald and Downland Open Air Museum at Singleton is devoted to the rescue and reconstruction of historic structures from all periods. Among those reconstituted are a market hall; a treadwheel; blacksmith's, carpenter's and plumber's workshops and a charcoal burner's camp: and there is also a modern reconstruction of a thirteenth century flint-rubble cottage, based on the remains of walls, oven and hearth excavated in the deserted village of Hangleton (Sussex). Winkhurst House, another of Singleton's buildings, is part of an actual cottage which may date back to the later fourteenth century, brought from Bough Beech, near Tonbridge (Kent). An attempt has been made to restore it to its original condition, though this is partly conjectural – it is not clear, for instance, whether it was originally thatched or tiled.

The house is of two bays, timber-framed with an infilling of wattle and daub: the floor is of beaten earth, and there is a central hearth, from which smoke escaped through a vent in the gable end. One bay is occupied by a solar reached by a staircase, and the house's glassless windows would have been closed with hides or shutters. It is not certain whether there were any service or farm outbuildings, but Winkhurst House bears some resemblance to the poor widow's cottage described by Chaucer in *The Nun's Priest's Tale*.

Singleton village is pleasant. The parish church of St John the Evangelist has an eleventh century tower and nave walls, while the chancel arcading has thirteenth century features, and much of the interior decoration is later medieval.

SINGLETON WEALD and DOWNLAND MUSEUM
West Sussex
OS 197 SU 870135
The fascinating open air museum is five and a half miles north of the cathedral city of Chichester, via the A286: immediately to the south are Goodwood Racecourse and the Trundle prehistoric hill fort.

Top left, the great hall of the 'Wealden House' is heated by an open fire, and above, the main entrance to the timber-framed building. Left, the Museum's first reconstruction, Winkhurst Farm, erected here in 1969.

SOUTHWELL MINSTER
Nottinghamshire
OS 120 SK 701538
Southwell (pronounced "Suth'l") is sixteen miles north-east of Nottingham via the A612, and six miles west of Newark (with its own fine church and castle) and the main A1 trunk road.

The minster was founded in 956; and by the early eleventh century it was a place of pilgrimage to the tomb of St Eadburgh. There is a pre-Conquest carving in low relief incorporated in the lintel over the door in the west wall of the north transept. The college of priests who served the Minster was under the patronage of the Archbishops of York, which probably helped to ensure the high quality of the design and workmanship in the post-Conquest rebuildings. At Southwell there is a striking contrast between the Norman and Gothic styles – both seen here at their best. The fine western towers, the nave, crossing and transepts are a rebuilding, on a cathedral-like scale, of the early twelfth century: while the choir is an ambitious replacement of 1233–48, showing how ribbed Gothic vaulting had transformed design, producing a new exuberance and harmony. There is a

fourteenth century stone choir screen with some humorously carved figures, and a profusion of fine stonecarving on both sides.

The Minster's naturalistic carvings, indeed, reach a peak of perfection: above all in the polygonal stone-vaulted chapter-house, dating from the end of the thirteenth century, built without a central pillar. The doorway leading to it from the vestibule is superb and the capitals feature some of the most sensitive leaf carvings in Britain, and there is more foliage sculpted on roof bosses and ribs. Remains of the Minster's medieval stained glass are in the windows of the chapter-house and in the south choir aisle.

Next to the Minster are the ruins of the palace of the Archbishops of York. The buildings were erected around a quadrangle in the later fourteenth century, and altered in 1439.

The choir of Southwell Minster is richly endowed with medieval carvings, in both wood and stone.

The chapter-house of Southwell Minster contains some of the very finest examples of medieval stone carving in the country.

Kings and Courtiers

After King John's loss of the Duchy of Normandy in 1204, the Kings of England perforce resided generally in their realm. Rebellions and the need to deal with the Scots and Welsh took them to the extremities of England, but they were most often to be found in its southern parts, especially at one of their houses in the Thames valley. This was a region they particularly liked because of its mild climate, good hunting country, ease of communications with the Continent (where they had vital interests) and nearness to the staple and luxury goods which the London markets could provide better than anywhere else in Britain. The growth of London as a trading centre freed kings and their households from the earlier necessity of moving from one group of royal estates to another, to subsist on their resources and on food levies from neighbouring lands. But kings kept up the habit of travelling a good deal, partly to facilitate cleaning and renovation in their palaces, partly to reduce expenses by short stays in abbey guest houses and magnates' castles, and partly to be seen by their subjects. In the summer, if they were not on campaign, kings liked to go on the equivalent of a modern holiday – hunting with close friends, visiting shrines and viewing their often curious relics perhaps in the spirit of a tourist as well as a pilgrim. During the autumn, winter, and spring, however, they often stayed at one of their principal residences for months at a time. Autumn was a time for council or parliament, Christmas for solemn public festivities and fun and games with nobles and courtiers before the gloom of the Lenten fast. Easter was another great court occasion, in the midst of a period when plans for the summer were made in council and parliament.

Kings therefore took measures to improve amenities at a few favourite principal residences where they were accustomed to make long stays with their households. They were concerned to add more spacious suites of private apartments, with amenities such as bath houses: thus Henry III turned Westminster into a luxurious residence, and Edward III did the same with Windsor Castle. Yet English kings also liked to escape from the bustle and tensions of the court with a few companions to private hunting-lodges: and the ballad-singers' tales of disguised or unrecognised princes moving among the people had some factual basis.

The English royal household was an almost entirely masculine organisation, as were other great households. Temporary laundresses might receive wages, but the only permanent female household officers were the companions (*domicellae* or "damsels") of queens, and the wet nurses, cradle-rockers and governesses of royal infants and small children. The household had a large number of distinct departments with their own internal hierarchies, many of them "below stairs" departments concerned with the storage, preparation and elaborate serving of food and drink: and there were also officers charged with the provision of fuel and furnishings; the keeping of the king's horses, falcons, and hounds; of transport vehicles, and of barges for use on the Thames. There were the dean, clerks and choristers of the Chapel Royal, who celebrated the liturgies publicly with fitting splendour, especially on the great Christian festivals when the king ceremonially wore his crown.

There were officers who served the king's personal needs, and who had the duty of attendance on him; there were close kinsfolk in residence and distinguished guests in suites of private apartments; while the clerk of the wardrobe and his staff safeguarded the king's personal treasures and movable wealth.

This clerk, with the steward of the household, the king's knights and squires, and his confessor, might be among the royal familiars who played significant parts in policy-making and government. They were among the élite of household officers who were easily available for consultation by the king – such men might help in drafting his correspondence, be sent on delicate political and diplomatic missions, or be entrusted with financing a campaign. This kind of service was a highway to promotion to some of the great offices of state, such as the chancellorship, or the treasurership of the Exchequer. These great officers and other royal councillors were expected to reside frequently in the royal household, wherever it travelled. But as a result of the spectacular growth of central bureaucracy and record-keeping in England in the thirteenth century, by the end of our period some government departments and courts had permanent offices in Westminster Palace. The Exchequer was there, and so were some of the Chancery clerks: and the courts of King's Bench and Common Pleas invariably met in Westminster Hall.

Princely courts were irresistible magnets to all manner of folk. In England poor people came hoping to benefit from the holiness of kingship, a growing concept in the thirteenth century: for there was a belief that the king's touch and the rings which he had blessed had curative powers, and these powers were exercised at formal ceremonies. Petitioners for pardons and favours also flocked to the court, hoping to attract the interest of those in daily contact with the king. Leading nobles were expected to reside regularly at court, where they were allotted suites; by praying, eating and playing with the king they re-affirmed the familiar bonds between Crown and nobility. Such nobles also expected to be summoned formally to give their counsel and assent on policy matters.

The court was, therefore, the principal political arena, where men sought (often in factious alliance) to compete for offices close to the king's person; and where those in such offices intrigued on behalf of themselves and their friends for further advancement and the fruits of royal patronage. The king's familiars sometimes represented the interests at court of particular magnates, but more often their favoured position provoked political crises: for magnates feared that bureaucrats were unsympathetic to their interests, and that they and the king's everyday companions were usurping the "natural" role of the magnates as the advisers of the Crown.

For many, then, the court was the most rewarding, frustrating, exciting place in the realm, a steamy reflection of the personal authority of kings whose needs it was designed to fulfil and whose authority it helped to enforce. Yet it was also an institution which was coming under increasing suspicion as wasteful, oppressive, and immoral; a place where unworthy adventurers might make their fortunes at the expense of the community.

STAMFORD Lincolnshire
OS 141 TF 030070
*The delightful stone-built town of
Stamford is just off the main A1 road,
about a hundred miles north of
London and thus an ideal resting
place for travellers to the north. Its
medieval buildings are concentrated
into a comparatively small area in the
town centre, while just to the south
(off the B1081 access road to the A1)
is Elizabethan Burghley House, open
from April until October. The village of
Tickencote, three miles to the north-
east and by the A1, has an
outstanding Norman church.*

A ford over the river Welland, on a main route between London and York, helped to make Stamford an important communications centre long before the Norman Conquest. It was one of the confederation of Midland boroughs which became a centre of Danish power in the late ninth century, and reached the height of its prosperity and expansion in the twelfth and thirteenth centuries. Bolts of cloth known as "Stamfords" were familiar as far away as Genoa by 1200. But by the mid-fourteenth century Stamford's cloth guild was complaining of falling membership: rural cloth-making was undermining the more restrictive urban centres of production.

Stamford has also always been an important strategic town. Here the barons who rose against King John in 1215 assembled before the sealing of Magna Carta: and in 1469 Edward IV concentrated his army here before facing the Lincolnshire rebels at "Losecoat Field", where the peasant insurgents soon broke under the bombardment of his guns. In 1536 the Duke of Suffolk held Stamford for Henry VIII, to guard against Lincolnshire rebels protesting about religious change. There are few traces left of the royal castle and town walls and most of the medieval religious houses have disappeared, but Stamford still has many fine early buildings. The parish church of All Saints is mainly thirteenth century, with fifteenth century window insertions and additions, such as the steeple and north chapel. Among its brasses are those of the clothiers John Browne (d.1442) and William Browne (d.1489) and their wives. William was the founder of Browne's Hospital (an almshouse in Broad Street whose contemporary buildings survive) and the woolpacks at his feet and

Above left, the west end of the south aisle, and above, exterior arcading on the south-facing wall of All Saints church.

those of John Browne and his wife indicate the source of their wealth. St Mary's parish church, nearby, has a thirteenth century tower but is mainly a rebuilding of the fifteenth century, as are St George's, St John the Baptist's and St Martin's parish churches. In St Martin's is the huge and opulent tomb of William Cecil, Lord Burghley (d.1598), Queen Elizabeth's principal minister: and just outside Stamford is his Burghley House, one of the finest surviving Elizabethan country houses.

See **Magna Carta and the Beginnings of Parliament.**

STOKE D'ABERNON CHURCH Surrey
OS 187 TQ 129585

The church stands about a mile south-east of Stoke d'Abernon, by the A245 road to Leatherhead. Some twenty miles south-west of central London, Stoke d'Abernon may be reached from there via the A3, turning east onto the A245 at Cobham: from the south or west, it is accessible via junction 10 of the M25, the A3 north, and the A245.

Parts of the structure of the parish church of St Mary date from before the Norman Conquest, but interior features in the nave and chancel testify to extensive rebuilding in the twelfth and thirteenth centuries. The Norbury Chapel was built in about 1490. It has a fireplace to warm the chantry priest – an unusual feature which was probably built for the comfort of John Pinnoke (d.1521), whom a brass plate on the east wall records as its first priest.

On the chancel floor is a slab about eight feet long with the life-size brass of Sir John D'Aubernoun (1277), the oldest surviving brass in England. He is in chain mail from head to foot, with a long surcoat, belt with sword, and reinforced kneepads. He carries a shield and has a lance with pennon. The nearby brass of Sir John D'Aubernoun the younger (1327) shows how armour was developing. Although still basically mailed, the younger Sir John also has a close-fitting metal helmet, and his arms and legs are protected by plate armour.

The church (which has some fifteenth-century stained glass) is also rich in funeral monuments dating from the fifteenth century onwards. The brass to Elyn (d.1516), daughter of Sir Edmund and Jane Bray, is a reminder of the prevalence of infant mortality. Elyn is portrayed as a baby wrapped in swaddling clothes.

STOKESAY CASTLE Shropshire
OS 137 SO 436818

The delightful castle stands by the A49 near Craven Arms, eight miles north-west of historic Ludlow: from April to September it is open on Wednesday and Saturday afternoon, during the winter on Saturday afternoons only. Just to the west is the little border town of Clun, with another castle, and picturesque hill country of the central Welsh Marches.

For much of the Middle Ages England had a prime, highly prized export commodity – wool. The revenues from customs on it were important in keeping kings financially afloat. In the later thirteenth century Italian merchants, backed by huge resources of liquid wealth, dominated this export trade, especially merchants of Florence and Lucca. But a few Englishmen were starting to amass fortunes in the trade, and among them were two Shropshire brothers, Nicholas and Laurence of Ludlow. In 1288 Laurence negotiated the purchase of the entire wool clip from an earl's extensive Surrey estates for the then vast sum of £400, and in 1294 he acted for Edward I in negotiating an extra levy on wool. In or before 1281 Laurence bought Stokesay, setting himself up in a manor-house as a country landowner: the Ludlow family were to live there for several hundred years. Laurence was not content with the existing house built by the Say family, minor gentlefolk – the lower storeys of the north tower may survive from this house, built around 1240. He erected the surviving hall, with the solar block at its south end and adjoining south tower; the north tower may have been renovated after his death in 1296. The courtyard was enclosed on the three other sides by a curtain wall, the whole surrounded by a moat: other domestic buildings, such as the kitchen along the north wall, have disappeared. An ornately carved timber gatehouse dating from the early seventeenth century gives entry to the courtyard.

The hall is stately, of four bays, with a central hearth and sets of externally gabled lancet windows, on the moat side as well as facing the courtyard; it has an openwork timber roof. An upper chamber of the solar block has two peepholes overlooking the hall: it was the moral duty of the lord as well as in his interest to see that the members of his household did not get into mischief. The pious Henry VI, for example, spied through peepholes on his servants in case they fell from grace through encountering the foolishness of visiting females.

The towers at either end of the residential block, with their small windows and their battlements, were capable of defence – indeed, a token resistance was made in the castle for the royalist cause in the Civil War. The tower's curious multangular design and re-entrant angles perhaps had a decorative as well as structural and defensive purposes. The southern tower in particular gives an eye-catching grandeur to what is essentially a fortified manor house – perhaps this reflects the taste of the *nouveau riche* Laurence of Ludlow and his family. He may have shared the sentiment inscribed in the windows of a house near Newark (Notts.) by a later wool merchant:

I thank God and ever shall
It is the sheepe hath payed for all.

Right, aspects of the castle at Stokesay.

SWEETHEART ABBEY New
Abbey, Dumfries and Galloway
OS 84 NX 965663
*The abbey is in south-west Scotland,
on the A710 seven miles south of
Dumfries: just north of New Abbey
village is Shambellie House, with an
interesting collection of period
costumes.*

Dervorguilla (d.1289) was the eventual
inheritor of her father Alan's lordship of Galloway. She married John de Balliol, head of
one of the leading Anglo-Norman families in
Scotland, which had been granted its estates
by David I in the twelfth century. Dervorguilla
was well-known for her pious benefactions.
After her husband's death she completed his
foundation of Balliol College, Oxford, to provide a corporate endowment for a group of
university masters. She was also responsible
for the building of the bridge which still spans
the fast-flowing river Nith at Dumfries; and
in 1273 she founded the Cistercian
monastery of Sweetheart in Nithsdale – an
old-fashioned and costly project. Sweetheart
was set up as a cell of Dundrennan Abbey
near Kirkcudbright, and was so called
because Dervorguilla had been so attached
to her husband Balliol that after his death she
kept his heart with her, embalmed and
enclosed in an ivory casket bound with silver.
There was a fashion for burying hearts and
other organs separately from bodies – thus,
though Henry III (d.1272) was buried in
Westminster Abbey, his heart was sent to Fontevrault Abbey in France. But it was unusual
to keep a heart like a relic among one's personal possessions. Dervorguilla had her
husband's heart buried with her before the
High Altar in Sweetheart Abbey. Her tomb
has disappeared, but there are remains in the
south transept chapel of its sixteenth-century
replacement. This has carved on it a somewhat squat effigy of Dervorguilla, clasping a
heart-shaped casket suspended from a chain
round her neck.

In 1292 Edward I recognised Dervorguilla's
son John Balliol as King of Scots. But his
revolt against Edward's overlordship in 1295
and the English invasion and deposition of
Balliol in the following year set off the Scottish Wars of Independence, and Sweetheart
Abbey, just across the Solway Firth from England, was vulnerable. Edward I stayed there
in 1300, returning from an invasion of Galloway, and in 1306 the abbot petitioned him
for £400 worth of compensation for dama-
ges caused by his Welsh soldiers. Before
1381 the buildings were also damaged by
lightning. In the sixteenth century the monks
looked to the protection of the most powerful
local family, the Maxwells, who got control of
their properties: and monastic life gradually
petered out. Yet the last abbot, the persistent
and elusive Gilbert Broun, intermittently
maintained Catholic worship here into his old
age. In 1609, when his chamber door was
broken down, there were found "a great
number of Popish books, copes, chalices, pic-
tures, images and such other Popish trash".

There are few remaining traces of the
monastic buildings, apart from the well-
preserved precinct wall. The church itself is
an impressive ruin, built in vivid red sandstone: it dates from the thirteenth century. It
has rose windows at the west and east ends;
but apart from these the church seems to
have ben built in the austere style which
reflected the Cistercians' distrust of the
ornate.

The adjacent village of New Abbey is a
pretty spot, with a restored eighteenth-
century water mill.

TEWKESBURY
Gloucestershire
OS 150 SO 889324
*Ten miles north of Gloucester, Tewkes-
bury is most easily reached via the
immediately adjacent exit 9 of the M5
motorway: the abbey church is to the
south of the attractive small town,
near the river Avon. Some three miles
south of Tewkesbury (via the A38 and
the B4213) is Deerhurst, with its
unusually large Anglo-Saxon church
(870300) and nearby Odda's Chapel:
and to the north-west are the Malvern
Hills.*

Tewkesbury boasts the second largest parish church in England: at the dissolution of the Benedictine abbey in 1539 the townsmen purchased the abbey church for their own use for £453. It had been an early Anglo-Saxon monastic site, but there are no identifiable remains of the pre-Conquest buildings, for in 1092 Robert Fitz Hamon, Norman lord of the manor, practically refounded the monastery. A rebuilding was completed in c.1121: and much of this stately church remains. The nave's rows of high simple columns have a solemn effect, contrasting with the vibrant wooden lierne vault above them, dating from the fourteenth century. A fire in 1205 led to the gradual rebuilding of the eastern parts of the church, with a chevet of chapels radiating from the presbytery aisles. The choir is a superb example of early fourteenth century work in the decorated style. Its eastern windows contain one of the finest existing collections of fourteenth century stained glass, with figures and coats of arms of the Clare and Despenser families, lords of the manor, patrons of the monastery and donors for its building works.

The abbey is rich in tombs, effigies and chantry chapels of the fourteenth and fifteenth centuries, and among them are those of Hugh Despenser and Elizabeth his wife. Hugh was the son of Edward II's greedy and unfortunate favourite: Elizabeth was a considerable benefactress to the abbey, who paid for some of the new windows. Here also is the chantry and tomb of Edward Lord Despenser (d.1375) and his wife. He was a great warrior, who went with the Black Prince to Gascony in 1335 and took part in his hard-fought victory at Poitiers in 1356. In the late 1360s he campaigned in Italy, where he won

Left, the alabaster effigies of Hugh Despenser and his wife Elizabeth Montacute in their ornately carved tomb. Above, the abbey is the second largest parish church in England.

107

The wonderfully elaborate vault over the sanctuary in Tewkesbury Abbey.

a great reputation, and in 1373–4 he was constable of the army with which John of Gaunt traversed France from Calais to Bordeaux, a gruelling feat which must have taxed Despenser's disciplinary abilities. Above his chantry (with its early fan vault) is an unusual kneeling effigy – Despenser in his armour, with traces of the original colouring and gilding. Nearby is the tomb of Despenser's fellow Knight of the Garter, Guy Lord Brian (d.1390), who fought for Edward III at Crécy in 1346 and was much employed by him as diplomat, administrator and soldier. But the most famous person to be buried in the abbey in the Middle Ages lacked the solid reputation earned by Brian and Despenser – Shakespeare's "false, perjur'd, fickle Clarence", brother of Edward IV and Richard III. Clarence was condemned for treason against Edward in 1478; and soon after his

death it was rumoured that he had died by drowning in a butt of malmsey wine (a Greek wine so named from Monemvasia in the Morea). His biographer, Dr Michael Hicks, is sceptical of the tale, whose only claims to conviction are that it is bizarre, and inexplicable in terms of propaganda. In the Clarence Vault bones which may be those of the duke and his wife (Warwick "the Kingmaker's" daughter Isabella) are preserved in a glass case.

Clarence had fought in 1471 alongside his brothers in the battle of Tewkesbury, which took place near the abbey. This victory for Edward IV and his supporters practically finished off the Lancastrian cause, not least because Henry VI's bellicose young son Edward Prince of Wales was killed in it. Lancastrian fugitives were slaughtered in the abbey precincts; even those who took refuge in the abbey church itself were dragged out, and many nobles were executed immediately as traitors taken in open rebellion. The inner side of the door to the abbey church's sacristy is covered with plates reputed to come from armour worn in battle.

There are few remains to be seen of the conventual buildings, but at the west end of the church is Abbey House, the residence of the abbots built in the fifteenth century, and there is also the heavily restored abbot's gatehouse. The small town is well worth visiting for its picturesque profusion of half-timbered houses.

THORNHAM PARVA Suffolk
OS 155 TM 109728
Thornham Parva is in northern Suffolk, roughly midway between Stowmarket and Diss and some twenty-two miles south of Norwich. The church is west of the village, which is on the A140 Diss–Ipswich road, immediately south of Yaxley.

At the far end of the nave is the fourteenth century retable, a fine and rare example of English panel painting of the period.

The parish church of St Mary has Norman doors and a chancel with early fourteenth century decorative features. The church is notable for two things – it is thatched, and it houses the Thornham Parva Retable (the back panel of an altar). The retable was discovered in 1927 and is unlikely to have been made originally for this church: dating from the first decades of the fourteenth century, it is a rare example of English painting of the period. It consists of nine upright panels, framed in three sections. The figures portrayed, from left to right, are St Dominic, St Catherine, St John the Baptist, the Crucifixion with the Virgin Mary, St John the Evangelist and St Paul; St Edmund, St Margaret of Antioch and St Peter. The retable is likely to have been made for a Dominican friary: and the inclusion of St Edmund suggests that this was an East Anglian house. There is great delicacy of line and strength of composition in the painting, especially in the folding of the drapery on the figures. The suffering shown in the figure of Christ and the reactions of the bystanders reflect what was to become a popular meditative theme – but St Edmund has elegantly curled hair. The intense religious sentiment combined with courtly tastefulness in the painting perhaps stem from the Dominican milieu: for that Order was much patronised by the nobility.
See **Bury St Edmunds.**

THORNTON ABBEY
Humberside
OS 113 TA 115190

The impressive abbey gatehouse is remotely situated near the Humber estuary, some ten miles east of Scunthorpe via the M180, A180, A160 and a minor road through Killingholme. From Hull and east Yorkshire it can be reached via the Humber Bridge, Barton-upon-Humber (with its Saxon church) and the A1077, turning east at Thornton Curtis.

Thornton Abbey was a house of Augustinian canons founded by William Count of Aumale in 1139. It was well-to-do; the prior and twenty-seven canons signed the deed of surrender at its dissolution in 1539. A general rebuilding had begun in the 1260s and continued into the fourteenth century: and the Lady Chapel at the east end of the choir was built in the early fifteenth century. Little, except foundations, remains of the church and monastic buildings: but Thornton Abbey has perhaps the most imposing monastic gatehouse still standing in England. The abbot had a royal licence to fortify in 1382, and the gatehouse was built mainly of brick, partly faced in stone: the moat in front of it, its vast size and the blank outside facade make clear that the gatehouse was intended as a serious defensive structure, as do the portcullis groove and arrow-slits. The front is

divided into five sections by two sets of turrets, and these and the spaces beween are liberally supplied with arrow-slits. Its fortress-like appearance, however, is softened by statue niches: and the three central sculptures over the vaulted archway – of St John the Baptist, the Coronation of the Virgin and St Augustine – remain. On the inside, the gatehouse presents a more domestic aspect (it was probably the abbot's lodging) and the great chamber on the first floor has an oriel window: but four projecting towers with small windows show that defence was kept in mind. In the late fifteenth or early sixteenth century, moreover, the gatehouse was strengthened by the addition of a long brick barbican ending in round towers. Who were the canons afraid of? Possibly they had bad relations with their tenants, but it is more likely that they feared incursions from sea raiders.

TINTERN ABBEY Gwent
OS 162 SO 533000

The abbey stands in the wooded gorge of the Wye Valley, midway between Chepstow and Monmouth on the winding A466, one of the prettiest roads in Britain. The countryside in every direction is delightful, and just to the west (across the Wye via Brockweir) is Offa's Dyke Path, St Briavel's Castle and the Forest of Dean.

Tintern Abbey, lying on a spit of flat meadowland in a curve of the deeply cut and wooded valley of the river Wye, has one of the prettiest settings of any monastic ruin in Britain: and the beauty of the church complements its romantic surroundings. Tintern was the first Cistercian foundation in Wales, colonised from L'Aumône (in the French diocese of Chartres) in 1131, and the land was given by Walter Fitz Richard, lord of *Chepstow.* The Cistercians' devout austerity attracted liberal endowments; their colonisation of the wilderness in a period of agrarian expansion multiplied their wealth, especially through pastoral farming. Tintern was no exception. The rigid and exclusive ideals of the Cistercians, however, combined with their increasing prosperity, made them enemies (such as the secular cleric Walter Map) in the late twelfth century. Map says that the monks

at Tintern had a man hanged at Woolaston and buried in the sand: "the poor wretch had stolen in after their apples, and found eternal rest at the hands of the brethren". But the monks continued to have admirers, such as the wealthy and influential Roger Bigod, Earl of Norfolk from 1270 to 1306: and Bigod helped to finance a rebuilding of the abbey church whose extensive ruins remain.

This has an aisled nave of six bays and an aisled choir of four bays with a rectangular east end: its transepts have two bays each. The tracery of some of the principal windows remains: that in the great east and west windows is particularly fine. There are also considerable remains of the conventual buildings, whose reconstruction was accomplished after the completion of the new church. This ambitious building programme seems to have strained the financial resources of the abbey in the early fourteenth century and may have led the monks to press heavily on their tenants, provoking hostility. Dr Cowley cites the cases of Philip Riband, brought before one of the abbey's manorial courts in 1340 "for the divers transgressions he had committed and for the contemptuous and arrogant words he had spoken against the abbot and monks". Such tenants did not look on the abbey with the admiring eye of William Worcestre, an early antiquary who visited it over a century later, and noted Roger Bigod's coat of arms in the great east window of the church. To some, then, the beauty of Cistercian architecture did not signify holiness but oppression.

See **Chepstow.**

Above, Tintern Abbey by the river Wye, and left, a profusion of medieval pillars and arches at the crossing.

TROTTON CHURCH
West Sussex
OS 197 SU 836225

The church and tiny village of Trotton stands by the river Rother and the A272, six miles east of Petersfield and the main A3 London–Portsmouth road. Just to the south are the South Downs, here heavily wooded.

The parish church of St George, in the pleasant valley of the river Rother, dates mainly from c.1300, except for the tower, (which is somewhat earlier). It is a rather plain building, inside as well as out. The west wall of the interior, however, has well-preserved wall paintings which have been dated to c.1380, and these lively and homely figures give a good impression of everyday life at the time when the poet Geoffrey Chaucer was in his prime. There are representations of Moses and Christ, the Carnal man with the Seven Deadly Sins and the Spiritual Man with the Seven Works of Mercy. The church also contains notable brasses. That of Margaret Camoys, c.1310 (who inherited the manor of Trotton) is the earliest surviving English brass of a woman. Her wimple and coverchief show the antecedents of the headgear since traditionally worn by nuns, though the ornamental fillet holding her hair in place strikes a less austere note. Her sleeves, emerging from a loose overgarment, are elegantly buttoned, and a lap dog slinks between her feet. The brass of Thomas Lord Camoys (d.1420) and his wife Elizabeth is one of the best preserved in England.

Camoys had a distinguished military career, culminating in his command in 1415 of the left wing of Henry V's army at the battle of Agincourt. The brass splendidly represents the sort of plate armour he would have worn then. He and his second wife clasp their right hands affectionately, and she makes an elegant gesture with her left hand. Here we see a courtly lady of royal descent, the widow of an earl's son – Sir Henry Percy, immortalised as "Hotspur" (a contemporary nickname) in the first part of Shakespeare's *King Henry IV*. Lady Camoys is fashionably attired in a gown calculated to show off her figure, and wears elaborate headgear, the kind which preachers were fond of denouncing. A tiny schoolboyish figure stands at her feet. Unlike Hotspur, who died fighting as a rebel against Henry IV at the battle of Shrewsbury in 1403, her second husband Lord Camoys was a staunch Lancastrian. He wears the collar of linked esses (SSS) which was a badge of Henry IV and Henry V: and, below the left knee, the insignia of the Order of the Garter, to which he was elected in 1416.

WELLS Somerset
OS 183 ST 552458

The small and attractive city of Wells is some twenty miles south of Bristol (via the A37 and A39), nineteen miles south-west of Bath and six miles north-east of famous Glastonbury. Nearby are the Mendip Hills, with Wookey Hole Cavern immediately to the north and the picturesque Cheddar Gorge some ten miles to the north-east, via the A371.

King Ine of Wessex, on the advice of St Aldhelm, is said to have founded a church here in c.705. In 909 the church became the seat of a bishopric, but after the Norman Conquest, in William Rufus's reign, there was a move to transfer the diocese to Bath. Bishop Robert of Lewes (1156–66) compromised by making Bath and Wells a joint bishopric, and this compromise eventually received papal confirmation in the thirteenth century.

Nothing visible, however, remains of the Anglo-Saxon church, and very little of its Norman successor, consecrated in 1148. The building of the present cathedral was probably initiated in the episcopate of Reginald de Bohun, c.1184–6; and it was consecrated in 1239. Its west front is a dramatic tour de force, reminiscent in its richness of design of some of the contemporary cathedrals in the Ile de France. The facade is divided into five sections by heavily projecting buttresses which, above a continuous arcade, have tiers of statues: the west front, in fact, has nearly 300 figures – angels, prophets, saints, and kings. The twin towers, built in the late fourteenth and early fifteenth centuries, with their more austere Perpendicular mouldings, offset the exuberance of the thirteenth century design.

The Lady Chapel was built to the east of the cathedral in the early fourteenth century (it has fragments of stained glass) and the central tower was then heightened. But since the extra weight threatened a collapse, during the episcopate of Ralph of Shrewsbury (1329–63) the huge strainer arches were inserted, a striking and attractive feature of Wells. During Bishop Ralph's time the three

Left, statues crowd the north-west corner of the cathedral church. Below, the west front is home to some 400 figures.

eastern bays of the choir were also completed, and the cathedral was linked to the Lady Chapel by the retrochoir.

There are finely sculpted thirteenth century effigies of bishops in the cathedral, as well as later medievel chantries and tombs of ecclesiastics. The most remarkable interior furnishing of the cathedral, however, is the clock in the north transept, which was in existence by 1392. The clock face is in fact a working astronomical model, which illustrates the medieval concept of the universe. On a little platform above it are the figures of four knights on horseback, who charge each other on the hour, one getting knocked over. In the triforium is a seated civilian figure (known as Jack Blandifer) who strikes bells with his heels at the hours and quarters, and on the hour strikes a bell with a hammer: with each stroke of the hour bell he also cocks his head. There is likewise a clock on the outside of the north transept, above which are two quarter-jacks, finely carved oaken figures four feet high. They wear full sets of plate armour of the late fifteenth century.

Wells Cathedral probably has the best preserved subsidiary medieval buildings of any English secular cathedral. There are the cloisters, with the library built over the east cloister in the fifteenth century, and there is the vaulted staircase with its clustered pillars leading from the north transept. This staircase bifurcates, one branch part of the way up leading off to the right to the thirteenth century chapter-house, through its vestibule where petitioners waited. This is a beautiful chapter-house, with delicately carved canopies over the wall seats, and a central pil-

lar whose ribs burst out like a flower to meet those springing from the wall pillars.

Past the diversion to the chapter-house, the staircase continues up to a gallery leading across the road, part of the Chain Gate built in the fifteenth century by Bishop Beckington so that the Vicars Choral, processing to and from the cathedral to chant the liturgies, should not be distracted by street life. At the other end of the Chain Gate is the hall built for the vicars to dine in by Bishop Shrewsbury in 1348. He also had the houses built for them which still form "Vicars Close", with their chapel at the opposite end, over which Beckington added a library for them.

To the south of the cathedral is the Bishop's Palace. The oldest part of this is the central block built in 1230–40 by Bishop Jocelyn, which was heavily restored in the nineteenth century. To the north is a domestic block built by Bishop Beckington (1443–65) and to the south the chapel and ruined great hall built by Bishop Burnell (1275–93). The outer defensive wall, gate-house, towers and moat were constructed in c.1340 by Bishop Shrewsbury. In the Long Gallery in the central block is the chair in which Whiting, the last Abbot of Glastonbury, is said to have sat at his trial in the nearby Banqueting Hall; and another with the name James Arthur carved on it – he was one of the monks executed with the abbot. The Bishop's Palace is best known from a habit of the swans on its moat; they ring a bell to be fed.

See **Acton Burnell, Glastonbury.**

Left, the central pillar in the chapter-house with its fan vaulting, and below, the medieval staircase, chapter-house to the right, leads on to Vicar's Close.

Visions of God and the Devil – the Church and Medieval Society

In the century or so before the start of our period relations between the Church and secular society had been revolutionised. The papacy had asserted its headship (under Christ) of Christendom, (a headship which had secular as well as spiritual dimensions) and was attempting to discipline society according to the rules of a rapidly evolving canon law and a proliferating hierarchy of ecclesiastical councils and courts. Among the most important principles of reform were that the Church should be a unified and autonomous institution, freed from the corrupting constraints of lay control which had so disfigured it: and that the clergy should form a distinct estate subject only to the control of the Church, and disciplined to a self-abnegating way of life, educated to a specialist vocation. The attempts to reform the secular clergy and the laity were paralleled by a movement to reform religious congregations and found new ones – there was a proliferation of variations on the Benedictine Rule for monks, while houses of canons adopted the Rule known as that of St Augustine.

It is safe to assume that by the start of our period the higher clergy were generally literate in Latin and had a good grasp of the precepts of the Gospels and the Church Fathers, and of the decrees of the general councils of the Church and canon law. It can safely be assumed too that knowledge of this sound basis for the Christian life had percolated to the laity.

One effect of this awareness was to highlight the contrast between the reformed model of Christian life and the reality of society. Among the secular aristocracy, for instance, the cult of chivalry idealised the casual shedding of the blood of fellow Christians – even for sport. Tournaments in northern France during the twelfth century were effectively pitched battles, as appears from the poem written about the life of William the Marshal, Earl of Pembroke (d.1219), who in his youth had been a famous jouster. But though general councils of the Church had condemned such "sports", and though participants risked excommunication, the old earl reminisced joyfully about his exploits.

The new aristocratic cult of courtly love also contained elements repugnant to the Church: for the romances often idealised an almost idolatrous love for another human, encouraging a flow of emotions more properly directed to Christ and His Mother; and they frequently endorsed relationships which were adulterous in intent if not in deed. The rise of towns and trade also encouraged a sinful way of life. For the sake of profit, merchants and craftsmen were often tempted to work on Sundays and holidays; while some merchants committed the sin of usury. Neither were the clergy freed from secular taints, for great clerks were now busy royal or baronial administrators, much concerned with worldly business and the rigid enforcement of their lords' rights.

For the conscientious and the devout, therefore, it appeared difficult to live in the world and not be corrupted by it. The pains of Hell were vivid in mens' minds (as the many surviving representations of them remind us) and the devils that appeared in the medieval imagination were horrifying extra-terrestrial creatures. Yet they might literally assume the guise of a good fellow or a pretty girl met in a tavern. Scarcely less painful than Hell were the torments of Purgatory where, it was firmly believed, sinners not actually damned would have to endure long penance. Purgatory was becoming an increasing preoccupation in the thirteenth century, and in order to ease their passage through it, the prudent frequently endowed Masses for their souls after death – sometimes said in perpetuity by a succession of priests exclusively employed for that purpose. One aim of setting up perpetual charitable foundations, indeed, was to ensure the prayers of generations of almsmen, scholars or schoolboys. Fears of Hell and Purgatory also stimulated the proliferation of saints' cults during the period, leading to the building of more imposing shrines and settings for holy relics. Many of the companies of pilgrims moving in all directions were not merely going to give thanks for a temporal benefit or to pray for one, but rather to seek the intercession of the saint for the future welfare of their souls.

For the good of one's soul, a safer course was to opt out of the secular world altogether: and it was quite common in the twelfth century for ageing knights and ladies, once they had fulfilled their secular obligations, to retire into monasteries as monks or nuns. Individuals also went off into the woods and hills to live the life of hermits in huts and caves, or else moved into a cell attached to a parish church.

In the early thirteenth century the Franciscans and Dominicans, and then other orders of friars, established a new model of piety which proved a great counter-attraction to monasticism; layfolk flocked to patronise the friars, to become friars and to imitate their model of piety. The friars were drawn (in varying and often controversial degrees) to the ideal of living in apostolic poverty in the secular world, eschewing as far as possible the possession of property; living by begging, and ministering to the spiritual needs of the laity as confessors and preachers. Friaries are thus located in towns; friars were often given run-down or slum plots, which was all they required, and their early buildings therefore lack distinction. During the rest of our period friars retained the respect of rich and poor, though they encountered violent hostility from monks and secular clerks.

By the later fourteenth century, indeed, the example of the friars had created a new type of lay piety: for they had demonstrated that it was possible to live in the world and yet not be of it. The devout noble or merchant might dress, eat and generally live luxuriously, indulging in worldly business and pastimes, as his or her estate and avocation demanded. Nevertheless, interspersed with this, his or her day might have a liturgical pattern like a priest's with private Masses as well as public worship among other members of the household. Every day the devout lay person might set aside time for meditation on holy books, perhaps with a confessor, and might also carry out private abstinences and austerities. Such individuals were developing an interior spiritual life amid worldly cares and distractions. But this reformation of the laity, so eagerly desired by early medieval reformers (and attained in ways which they could not have envisaged) held dangers for the Church. For secular life could now be made almost as religiously respectable as that of the clergy; by the high standards that some of the laity were now adopting, indeed, the lives of many monks and secular clerks were wanting. Layfolk were becoming learned in the Scriptures and developing individual concepts of communion with God.

*The charming little town of
Winchelsea is eight miles north-east of
Hastings and three miles south-west
of its fellow Cinque Port of Rye, on
the A259. The Pipewell Gate is to the
north of the town, Strand Gate to the
east, and New Gate some distance to
the south.*

Winchelsea was admitted as one of the
Cinque Ports in 1191. In the thirteenth century, however, it suffered damage as a result
of storm inundations, culminating in a great
storm in 1288, and Edward I provided a site
for a new town, 150 acres on high ground.
In the north part of this area plots were laid
out in a grid pattern of intersecting streets.
But this was one of the new towns which
never fulfilled expectations, and settlement
was confined to the north-east corner, in only
twelve of the original thirty-nine blocks. The
wide spaces between the present houses
there show how stunted the original urban
growth was. Most of these houses date from
the eighteenth century or later, but there are
over thirty cellars surviving from the later
thirteenth and early fourteenth centuries.
There are also remains of the new town's
ambitious public buildings – among them
three gatehouses (Strand Gate, Pipewell
Gate and New Gate) and the fourteenth-
century Court Hall, housing a museum about
the Cinque Ports. In Friars Road is the Greyfriars, principally the ruins of the chancel
(*c.*1310) of the Franciscan friary: this is a rare
survival in England of part of one of the
Order's medieval churches. Of the parish
church of St Thomas of Canterbury, only the
chancel, side chapels and ruined transepts
remain, dating from the early fourteenth century. The west porch and entrance are fifteenth century, and in the chapels there are
five tombs with effigies, dating from the early

fourteenth century. The two in the north
chapel may be of Gervase Alard (d.1310) and
Stephen Alard, admirals of the Cinque Ports.
See **Rye.**

*The parish church of St Thomas of
Canterbury.*

Before the Norman Conquest Winchester was one of the most important and prosperous towns in England. It had traditionally been a residence of the kings of Wessex; and they and their successors the kings of England continued to come there and endow its monasteries, including St Swithun's (the Old Minster), the seat of one of the richest English bishoprics. North of the present cathedral can be seen the outline of its predecessor, dating from the mid-seventh century. This was replaced by a Norman cathedral begun in 1079 during the episcopate of Bishop Walkelin: by 1093 it was sufficiently complete for the transference there of the relics of St Swithun, and in 1100 William Rufus was buried there: his plain tomb is in the choir. The principal remaining parts of the Norman church are the choir, central tower, transepts and crypt. The Norman east end was demolished during the episcopates of Bishops Lucy (1189–1204) and des Roches (1204–38) to make way for a retrochoir (terminating in chapels) to house St Swithun's shrine more fittingly and to provide a fine Lady Chapel. The original tiles remain in the retrochoir and its aisles, remarkably complete. In the fourteenth century more of the Norman church was reconstructed, by remodelling as well as demolition. Bishop Edington (d.1366) replaced the western Norman towers by a rather mechanically designed west front: the presbytery was also remodelled, and so was the nave, completed in

Bishop Wykeham's episcopate (1367–1404). Here the Norman triforia were scrapped and the main columns continued upwards to meet the vaulting ribs in a design of great dignity and coherence. Edington's and Wykeham's work comprise one of the earliest large-scale essays in the Perpendicular style (compare Edington's rebuilding of *Edington* church).

The cathedral has many notable furnishings and monuments. In the nave is a fine font of black Tournai marble, and the tombs and chantry chapels of Edington and Wykeham. The choir stalls (*c*.1308) are one of the earliest sets in England, with an array of foliage and animal carving in the spandrels, and of carvings of secular subjects under the misericords (two carved heads there having moving tongues). The stone screens round the choir, erected by Bishop Fox (*c*.1525), have on top of them mortuary chests containing the remains of Anglo-Saxon and Danish kings. The reredos dates from 1501–02; on it are the arms of Henry VII's short-lived son prince Arthur and his bride Catherine of Aragon. In the retrochoir are the chantry chapels of four bishops who all played important parts in politics and royal government – Cardinal Henry Beaufort (d.1447), Henry IV's half brother; William Waynflete (d.1486), founder of Magdalen College, Oxford; Richard Fox (d.1528), founder of Corpus Christi College, Oxford; and Stephen Gardiner (d. 1555), who married Mary Tudor

WINCHESTER Hampshire
OS 185 SU 483294
The ancient (though now much modernised) city of Winchester is some sixty-five miles south-west of London, via the M3 motorway. The cathedral and Bishop's Palace are near the centre of the city, and the castle hall (with its Round Table) are a short walk to the west via Great Minster Street, High Street, and Castle Avenue. To the south of the cathedral close is Winchester College (usually open all year) from which a rather longer journey down College Walk and across the water-meadows takes the pedestrian traveller to St Cross Hospital (also accessible by car from the A333, about a mile south of the city centre).

The west front of the cathedral.

119

Chantries in the retrochoir of Winchester Cathedral.

and Philip II of Spain in the cathedral.

There are some remnants of the cathedral priory's monastic buildings in the Cathedral Close: and to the south-east of the cathedral, in the grounds of the Bishop's Palace, are the ruins of the episcopal Wolvesey Castle. Outside the city's thirteenth century Westgate is a noble fragment of the royal castle – its great hall, a remnant of the palatial domestic building works which Henry III carried out at his residences. On its west wall hangs King Arthur's Round Table. This table was at Winchester, and known as "King Arthur's" by the fifteenth century: but recent research suggests that this massive piece of carpentry (painted with the Tudor rose and familiar cartwheel design in the sixteenth century) was put together in about 1330. Perhaps it was connected with the cult of King Arthur which the young Edward III revived at his court: if so, we may have here a genuine piece of Plantagenet court furniture.

In the centre of the medieval city is its marketcross, the High Cross, dating from the fifteenth century. By then the city had long since declined: it was no longer a great weaving centre (since the thirteenth century the new town of Salisbury had captured much of its long-distance trade) and it had ceased to be a favourite royal residence. Yet Winchester had become a remarkable educational centre, for in 1382 Bishop Wykeham founded his grammar school there, larger than any previous English school and a model for future foundations. Winchester College is beyond the medieval Kingsgate, to the south of the cathedral; its original collegiate buildings form the nucleus of the later school buildings.

Outside the medieval city (but within a modern suburb) is the Hospital of St Cross. The original foundation of an almshouse was made in 1136 by King Stephen's brother Henry of Blois, Bishop of Winchester: and in 1446 this was supplemented by Cardinal Beaufort's endowment of "The Almshouse of Noble Poverty". There is a fine twelfth-century church; and the brethren still live in the medieval quadrangle. Those of the original foundation wear black gowns with the cross of the crusading Order of the Knights Hospitaller (who administered the almshouse 1151–1303), while the "Beaufort Brothers" wear claret-coloured gowns and the cardinal's hat badge. The Wayfarer's Dole, a small horn of beer and a piece of white bread, is distributed daily from the hatchway of the porter's lodge.
See **Edington.**

York Minster, as it was rebuilt by the fifteenth century, was one of the biggest buildings in England. It was an apt expression of northerners' regional patriotism; its beauty stemmed in part from the donations lavished on it by local nobles and ecclesiastics, reflected in the coats of arms and figures of donors in its stained glass windows: these were produced by the York school of glass painters, many of whom had their workshops in nearby Stonegate. Thus the great west window was given by Archbishop Melton (1338) and in the north wall of the nave is a window given by Richard Tunnoc (d.1330), goldsmith and bellfounder: bells are a decorative motif in the window, which depicts the bellfounder's craft and Tunnoc himself offering a bell to St William of York.

The site of the minster had curious antecedents, for it lies athwart the remains of the military headquarters of the Roman legionary fortress of Eboracum. Hereabouts, in about 627, the missionary Paulinus, favourably received by King Edwin of Northumbria, set up a wooden church. An Anglo-Saxon stone successor was burnt in 1069 in one of the spectacular fires which have punctuated the Minster's history. This was replaced by an exceptionally large Norman church begun in around 1080: parts of its transepts – and of the Roman headquarters – can be seen in the Undercroft, a great hollow excavated in 1967–72 to insert underpinnings for the endangered crossing and fifteenth century central tower.

Another complete rebuilding, however, was undertaken from the early thirteenth century onwards: and this constitutes what we now see as the Minster. The transepts were built during the archiepiscopate of Walter de Gray, c.1220–55. His tomb is in the south transept, with an effigy showing him in his vestments, his staff thrust into a dragon's mouth. In 1968 the lid of the coffin was found to bear a life-sized painting of Gray, now in the Treasury in the Undercroft. In the north transept is the Five Sisters Window, five lights fifty feet high filled with geometric patterns of leaf and stem design painted on white glass. The effect is plain and austere, contrasting with the intense colour effects attained elsewhere in the Minster's glass – for instance,

Tomb of the child Prince William of Hatfield, son of Edward III.

YORK North Yorkshire
OS 105 SE 604524
The famous city of York is some two hundred miles north of London, via the A1 and A64, and is a major tourist centre. Its great Minster dominates the city, renowned for its Georgian and medieval buildings: and a short walk to the south is Clifford's Tower on its mound, which is immediately adjacent to the Castle Museum (with its roofed-over Victorian and Edwardian streets) and near both the Jorvik Viking Centre and the Merchant Adventurer's Hall in Fossgate. All Saints North Street, distinguished by its needle-pointed stone spire, is somewhat hidden away by the river, opposite the modern Viking Hotel.

in the later thirteenth century windows in the chapter-house.

In 1291 Archbishop Romanus laid the foundations of a new nave, whose constructions continued well into the fourteenth century. It has eight bays in the Decorated style; and each division of the triforium has five canopied arches. The spandrels between the arches bear the coats of arms of Edward II and the barons who attended the York parliament of 1309–10. All the high roof vaulting in the Minster is wooden. The choir screen, with its statues of English kings, is fifteenth century: and in the north choir aisle is the tomb and boyish effigy of Edward III's son William of Hatfield, who died young in 1344. The most spectacular window in the Minster

The nave of York Minster.

is the great east window, commissioned by the dean and chapter from John Thornton of Coventry and donated by Walter Skirlaw, Bishop of Durham (d.1408), who is depicted kneeling at an altar in the central lower panel. The patriotic focus of northern affection on the Minster made up for its lack of a famous shrine, though visitors came from afar to the tomb of St William (now in the crypt) and, in the fifteenth century there were unofficial cults there of an executed archbishop Richard Scrope (d.1405) and a murdered king, Henry VI (d.1471).

The chapter-house, entered from the north transept and dating from c.1280–c.1307, is an octagon with a pyramidal wooden roof. Its stalls have finely sculpted canopies supported by Purbeck marble shafts. The finest remaining domestic building of the medieval cathedral clergy is St William's College, a timber-framed quadrangular building immediately to the east of the Minster; it was founded in 1461 for the chaplains who served the cathedral altars.

Since Roman times York's strategic position has made it a vital base for anyone who wanted to dominate the North of England. The Norman kings raised a castle there between the rivers Ouse and Foss, whose mound remains. On it the persecuted Jews of York died amidst flames in 1190; the stone keep, Clifford's Tower, dates from the mid thirteenth century. The city walls and most of their gates (known as "bars") survive from this and the following century, one of the best preserved British medieval urban defence systems.

Medieval York flourished as a centre of the distributive trades, serving the needs of the rich Yorkshire magnates, clergy and gentry who treated it as a provincial capital. Workers in leather, cloth and metal were prominent there in the thirteenth century. A mercantile elite grew rich through handling Yorkshire wool exports, facilitated by the ease of navigation down the Ouse to Hull; and in 1357 York merchants were licensed by Edward III to form a fraternity and possess communal property. They built what is now the undercroft of the Merchant Adventurers' Hall, Fossgate: the building also has a chapel reconstructed in 1411 and a great hall dating from the same century.

Mercantile wealth is also reflected in York's profusion of finely built medieval parish churches and their stained glass. At All Saints, North Street (on the west bank of the Ouse), the windows of the north choir aisle have figures of donors and illustrations from a popular fourteenth century devotional tract, *The Prick of Conscience*.

GLOSSARY OF KINGS

HENRY II succeeded to the throne in 1154: he was the son of Geoffrey Count of Anjou and Matilda, daughter of Henry I. Because Henry II and his sons and successors Richard I and John were of the House of Anjou they are known as the "Angevin" kings. They ruled the western provinces of France as separate components of a vast "Angevin empire" which also included, besides the English kingship, claims to the overlordship of Wales, Scotland and Ireland. England tended to be a political backwater for much of Henry's long reign. He had little difficulty in restoring the traditionally strong royal authority there after the civil wars of his predecessor Stephen's reign. Henry strengthened the effectiveness and scope of the common law and increased the authority of his judges. This caused disputes with the Church, in which Henry met his most formidable opponent – his former chancellor Thomas Becket, who when Archbishop of Canterbury was murdered in his cathedral at Henry's instigation in 1170. But the one great baronial rebellion against Henry's rule (1173–4) soon petered out.

Henry spent much of his reign in France, upholding his authority in his numerous lordships and attempting to extend his rule. There he encountered the hostility of its kings, overlords of his French lands. They encouraged the grievances of his quarrelsome sons: it was in the midst of a rebellion by them that Henry died in 1189. Tomb effigies of Henry and his queen Eleanor of Aquitaine can be seen in Fontevrault Abbey in Anjou.

RICHARD I succeeded his father Henry II in 1189 and immediately set about organising an army to join the French and Germans on the Third Crusade, whose aim was to recover Jerusalem, captured from the westerners by the Muslims in 1187, to the shame of western Christendom. Richard set off in 1190: he secured Acre and Jaffa and defeated the Muslims in the battle of Arsuf, but his forces were not sufficiently strong to gain Jerusalem. He had to be content with making a truce with the Islamic leader Saladin, who much admired him. On Richard's journey home he was imprisoned in Germany: he was released in 1194 on payment of a huge ransom. Meanwhile problems were multiplying in his empire. His brother John stirred up tensions in England by challenging the rule of his deputy (justiciar) there. His overlord in France, Philip Augustus, encouraged dissidents there. But after his return Richard turned his formidable military talent to wage war against the French king. In 1199, during a minor siege, Richard was fatally injured by a crossbow bolt. He died childless and was buried near his parents in Fontevrault Abbey, where his tomb effigy can be seen.

JOHN succeeded his brother Richard I in 1199, though some of his French subjects would have preferred to have their nephew Arthur of Brittany as ruler. John gave the discontented in France an opportunity to strike against him by antagonising one of his important subjects in the provinces of Poitou, who complained about John's conduct to the French king, Philip Augustus. The latter used this as an excuse to declare John's territories in France forfeited. At first John was successful in defending them, capturing Arthur (who died in custody), but in 1204 Philip Augustus unhinged the defences of the lands north of the Loire by conquering Normandy. For the next ten years John strove to tap English resources and international support to recover his lost French lands. His attempts finally collapsed with the defeat of his continental allies at Bouvines (1214).

During the previous decade John had been the first Angevin king to rule in person for an extended period in England: he was a hard-working judge and administrator, whose distrust of his barons and enforcement of heavy fines earned him widespread hatred, more intense than that felt for the grasping rule of his brother and father. He became embroiled with the Church, which resulted in the imposition on England by Pope Innocent III of an Interdict suspending all religious services (1208–13). An alliance of barons took advantage of his defeat at Bouvines to launch a rebellion: John's concession of the comprehensive and humiliating Magna Carta (1215) was intended to defuse revolt. John soon repudiated the charter: civil war ensued, in which his opponents were supported by an invasion of England led by Philip Augustus's son Louis. John died suddenly in the midst of campaigning and is buried in Worcester Cathedral, where his effigy is to be seen on his tomb.

HENRY III succeeded his father John in 1217: he was then aged only nine and civil war was in progress. But this soon petered out: Henry's supporters won over opponents by re-issuing versions of Magna Carta. When a young man, Henry showed himself determined to assert his personal authority and to recover the lands in France lost by his father. But his rule provoked discontents. Local elites smarted at the efficiency of a royal administration over which they had no control and at royal financial demands. Magnates were affronted by Henry's favours to his and the queen's foreign kinsmen and were irritated by his inept adventures in diplomacy and war. In 1258–9 barons forced the financially embarrassed king to share control of government and drew up schemes for reform and for a permanent monitoring system. Henry sought help to restore his authority from Louis IX of France (St Louis) and in 1259, by the Treaty of Paris, made peace with the French Crown, abandoning claims to the lost lands in France and agreeing to hold the province still in his hands, the Duchy of Gascony, as a feudal vassal of Louis and his successors. But in England a formidable baronial protagonist frustrated Henry's efforts, his brother in law Simon de Montfort, Earl of Leicester, who captured the king at the battle of Lewes. In 1265 Montfort was defeated and killed at the battle of Evesham by Henry's son, the future Edward I. In the next few years baronial dissidence was overcome. Henry III died in 1272 and was buried in Westminster Abbey.

EDWARD I succeeded his father Henry III in 1272. Edward had the authoritarian temperament of his ancestors but was shrewder than his father and schooled in the lessons of civil war. Determined to restore royal authority and good order, he instituted inquiries into the rights by which landowners held their jurisdictions and thoroughly overhauled the civil and criminal law. He summoned representatives of shires and boroughs to some parliaments (meetings of the king with the principal men of the realm), in order to improve links between the Crown and the often disgruntled local communities and to commit them to support and implement his policies.

Edward was much concerned with asserting his claims to sovereignty over the whole of Britain: in 1277 he defeated Llywelyn Prince of Wales and in the early 1280s conquered his principality and annexed it to the English Crown. The Marches of Wales continued to be ruled by hereditary Anglo-Norman lords acknowledging the overlordship of the Crown. The dying out of the direct Scottish royal line in 1290 enabled Edward to press his claim to the overlordship of Scotland, but John Balliol, his choice as king, rebelled against his interference. In 1296 Edward invaded Scotland, deposed Balliol and commenced the English occupation. A knightly Balliol supporter, William Wallace, led a successful rebellion, but was decisively defeated by Edward at Falkirk in 1298. But a rival of the Balliols, Robert Bruce, whose grandfather had been a claimant to the throne, raised revolt, and was crowned king in 1306.

In 1294 Edward had become embroiled in war with his overlord, Philip IV of France, who was asserting himself in the affairs of Edward's Duchy of Gascony. The extortionate demands for services and money to fight Philip and to suppress Scottish resistance alienated his English subjects in his later years and provoked a resurgence of baronial opposition. Edward died in 1307 at Burgh on Sands (Cumbria), when preparing once again to invade Scotland, and was buried in Westminster Abbey.

EDWARD II succeeded his father Edward I in 1307. He was faced with pressing problems – the challenge in Scotland from Robert I (Robert Bruce), the simmering disputes with the French Crown over Gascony, and English grievances over the harsh and arbitrary government of his father's last years. Edward lacked the ability to deal with these problems. He failed to appease the barons by consultation or the community by curbing the activities of his officials. Magnates were incensed by the favours which he showered on a personable foreigner, Piers Gaveston. In 1310 Edward agreed to a degree of baronial control over government: Gaveston was lynched in 1312. Edward had made a dangerous opponent – his cousin Thomas Earl of Lancaster, the wealthiest and most influential magnate in the realm. In 1314 Edward lost his footholds in Scotland as a result of his crushing defeat at Bannockburn by Robert I. But he would not make peace with Robert and was unable to defend northern England against Scottish devastation. Edward antagonised the lords of the Welsh Marches by aggrandising the Despenser family. But the rebellion of Marcher lords in alliance with Thomas of Lancaster was defeated in 1322: Thomas was executed after being captured at the battle of Boroughbridge. The destruction of Edward's enemies and the reforming efficiency of his ministers failed to ensure stable rule, since his policies had agitated and alienated large sections of the political community. His own wife, Isabella of France, was one of his implacable enemies: in 1326 she invaded the realm with her lover, Roger Mortimer. Edward and the Despensers could not muster sufficient support: the Despensers were executed and the captured king was forced to abdicate in favour of his son Edward. An escape attempt appears to have precipitated Edward II's murder, though some contemporaries believed that he escaped abroad and died obscurely in Italy. His alleged tomb is in Gloucester Cathedral.

EDWARD III was one of the most successful English kings, despite – or perhaps because of – his father's deposition. In 1330 he overthrew the disgraceful rule of his mother, Isabella, and her lover, Roger Mortimer, Earl of March, and in 1333 reversed their sensible policy of peace with Scotland by invading it, reviving the ambitions of his grandfather Edward I. But Edward III's main foreign preoccupation from 1337 onwards was to be France, whose king, Philip VI, then declared his Duchy of Gascony forfeited. Lengthy war ensued, punctuated by truces: the enormous costs produced protests from Edward's subjects. These became muted when he eventually allowed the main war taxes to be negotiated with the representatives of the shire and borough communities in parliament, and showed himself sympathetic to a wide range of their grievances. He aroused enthusiasm for the war by engaging the chivalrous interests of the nobles in it and stirring up distrust and hatred of the French. Successes in the war brought profits to the participants. Edward won the battles of Sluis (1340) and Crécy (1346) and his son Edward Prince of Wales (the Black Prince) captured John II of France in his victory at Poitiers (1356). In 1360 Edward made peace, giving up the claim to the throne of France which he had flaunted since 1340 and receiving from John the Duchy of Aquitaine in full sovereignty. But in the long run the gains won by English tactical superiority could not be held against the concentration of superior French resources. In the war of 1369–75 John's son Charles V won back from Edward what had been conceded in 1360. Edward died in 1377, old, discredited, a shadow of his former self. He was buried in Westminster Abbey.

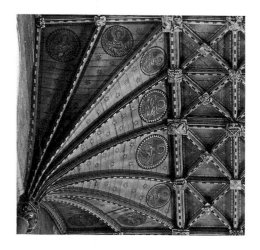

GLOSSARY OF TERMS

ABBEY An independent monastery ruled by its own abbot or abbess, as opposed to a dependent *priory*.

AISLES Where a *chancel*, *nave* or *transept* is divided up by rows of pillars, the aisles are the corridor-like sections flanking the central space.

ARCADE A row of arches, generally supported on pillars.

AUGUSTINIANS The oldest and largest order of *canons regular*, who followed the rule named after St Augustine of Hippo: they had more English houses than any other religious order.

BAILEY Walled enclosure of a castle, generally containing domestic and other buildings.

BARBICAN Outwork defending the entrance to a castle.

BAY Internal division of a building, separated from others by pillars etc. rather than solid walls.

BENEDICTINES The largest and earliest order of *monks*, founded by St Benedict of Nursia (d.550): also called "black monks", they owned many of the richest British monasteries.

BURGESS A substantial townsman, generally possessing various rights and privileges.

CANONS REGULAR Groups of priests following a monastic rule and living together in an *abbey* or *priory*: in practice almost indistinguishable from *monks*.

CANONS SECULAR Priests serving a *cathedral* or other great church, but owning individual property and neither bound by a monastic rule nor necessarily living communally.

CAPITALS Block-like heads of columns or pillars, often shaped or sculptured.

CATHEDRAL A great church which is the seat of a bishop or archbishop.

CHANCEL The part of the east end of a church where the main altar is placed, or sometimes the whole eastern half of the church. See also *choir*.

CHANTRY CHAPEL Chapel within or attached to a church, where masses were said for the souls of the chantry's founder and others.

CHAPTER HOUSE The building in a monastery or cathedral where the monks or cathedral clergy met to discuss business, and in the case of monks to hear a chapter of the monastic rule.

CHOIR Strictly, the part of a church where services are said or sung: but sometimes used as a synonym for *chancel*.

CISTERCIANS Order of *monks* following the austere reform of the *Benedictine* rule which originated at Cîteaux in France: stressing the importance of physical labour, these "white monks" grew rich by sheep-farming.

CLERESTORY Uppermost storey of a church wall, generally containing windows and thus a "clear-storey".

CLOISTER The courtyard of a monastery, often surrounded by a covered walk where the monks took exercise.

CLUNIACS Orders of *monks* following the reformed *Benedictine* rule established at Cluny (France): noted for the beauty and elaboration of their churches.

COLLEGIATE CHURCH A large church of less than *cathedral* status, served by a "college" of secular *canons*.

CORBELS Blocks of stone projecting from a wall, supporting the eaves of a roof or some other feature.

CROSSING Space near the centre of a church, where the *chancel*, *nave* and *transepts* meet. In larger churches, the area under the central tower.

CRYPT Underground chamber beneath a church, generally at its east end.

CURTAIN WALL Stretch of plain wall between the towers of a castle or other fortification.

DECORATED Style of Gothic architecture which flourished in England from c.1280 until c.1340.

EARLY ENGLISH Style of architecture (also called early Gothic) which flourished in England during the thirteenth century, from the end of the *Norman* period until c.1280.

EFFIGY Sculptured statue representing the deceased,

placed on a tomb or monument.

FACADE The "show front" of a building, adorned with statuary or other elaborate sculptured decoration.

FRIARS Members of the new religious orders inspired by St Francis in the thirteenth century, these "brothers" were vowed to absolute poverty, ministered to the poor, and lived by begging.

GARDEROBE A medieval privy or lavatory, often built into the thickness of a wall.

GRANGE An outlying farm belonging to and administered by a monastery.

GUILDS Fraternities, generally of townsfolk, with religious, social and (usually) commercial function: "guilds merchants" protected trade, while craft guilds regulated manufacturing industries.

KEEP The principal and innermost strongpoint of a castle, often a massive tower: from the thirteenth century onwards sometimes combined with a formidable gatehouse.

KNIGHT Originally a man holding land in return for personally serving as a mounted soldier in wartime, and who had knighthood ceremonially bestowed on him by the king or another great lord: later an honorific title, though the ceremonies continued.

LADY CHAPEL Chapel dedicated to the Virgin Mary, often at the east end of a church.

LAY BROTHERS Inferior grade of *monks*, generally uneducated and occupied with manual work.

MACHICOLATIONS *Corbels* at the head of a castle tower or wall, supporting an overhanging gallery from which projectiles could be dropped on attackers.

MOAT Ditch surrounding and protecting a castle or other fortification, sometimes but not always filled with water.

MONKS Men (not necessarily priests) living an enclosed life of poverty, chastity and obedience in a monastic *abbey* or *priory*.

MOTTE Artificial earthen mound forming the strongpoint of an early Norman castle, and sometimes topped by a *keep*.

NAVE Western section of a church, generally used to provide space for the congregation.

NORMAN Style of architecture current in England from 1066 until the late twelfth century: often called Romanesque in Scotland, where it continued rather later.

PERPENDICULAR Latest style of Gothic architecture, flourishing in England from *c.*1335 to *c.*1530 and in Scotland rather longer.

PRESBYTERY In greater churches, the section lying east of the *choir* and containing the high altar. So called because it was reserved for priests.

PRIORY A dependent monastery ruled by a prior or prioress, but technically subordinate to a greater *abbey*. Cathedral priories were so called because their nominal abbot was the bishop or archbishop.

ROMANESQUE See *Norman*.

ROOF BOSS A projection, often elaborately carved, placed at the intersection of the ribs of a roof *vault*.

SCREEN Decorative feature, often richly carved and pierced, dividing one part of a church (generally the *choir*) from another.

SEDILIA Seating by the altar, often of carved stone and built into a wall, for priests officiating at services.

SOLAR Private living room occupied by the owner of a castle or medieval house.

SQUIRE Either a young man training to be a *knight* or an adult gentleman of less than knightly rank.

STALLS Rows of permanent seating for priests or monks, generally of elaborately carved wood and placed in the *choir*.

TOWER HOUSE Compact fortified residence in the form of a tower, common in Scotland and northern England from the late thirteenth century onwards.

TRANSEPT The transverse projections, or "arms", of a cross-shaped church. Some very large churches have two sets of transepts, forming a "cross of Lorraine" plan.

UNDERCROFT Vaulted basement, often semi-subterranean.

VAULT An arched stone roof.

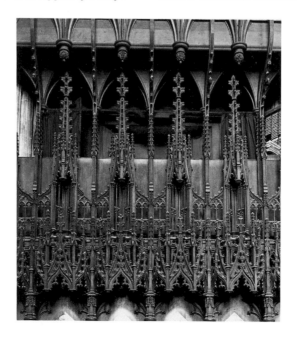

FURTHER READING

Anderson, M. D., *History and Imagery in British Churches*,
 John Murray, 1971
Baker, T., *Medieval London*, Cassell, 1970
Barrow, G. W. S., *Kingship and Unity. Scotland 1000–1306*,
 Edward Arnold, 1981
Brieger, P. H., *English Art 1216–1307*, Oxford, 1957
Clanchy, M. T., *England and its Rulers 1066–1272*, Fontana, 1983
Evans, J., *English Art 1307–1461*, Oxford, 1949
Harvey, J., *The Master Builders. Architecture in the Middle Ages*,
 Thames and Hudson, 1971
Platt, C., *The Castle in Medieval England and Wales*,
 Secker and Warburg, 1982
Prestwich, M., *The Three Edwards. War and State in England 1272–
 1377*, Weidenfeld and Nicolson, 1980
Stone, L., *Sculpture in Britain. The Middle Ages*, Penguin, 1972

The publishers would like to extend their thanks to the many individuals and organisations who have cooperated in the production of this book, including amongst others:

The Vicar and Church Wardens of Boston, the Dean of Bristol, CADW: Welsh Historic Monuments, the Dean and Chapter of Canterbury, English Heritage, the Vicar of Dorchester, the Vicar of Elsing, the Master of the Temple Church, London, Much Marcle Parochial Church Council, the Dean of Peterborough, the Dean of Ripon, the Dean of Salisbury, Scottish Development Department, the Director of the Weald and Downland Open Air Museum at Singleton, the Provost of Southwell, the Vicar of Stamford, the Vicar and Church Wardens of Tewkesbury, the Dean and Chapter of Wells, the Dean and Chapter of Winchester, and the Dean and Chapter of York.

English Heritage, The National Trust, the Department of the Environment, CADW: Welsh Historic Monuments, and the Scottish Development Department are all official bodies entrusted with responsibility for maintaining particular places and structures for the benefit of travellers, now and in the future.

Membership of one or more of these organisations is strongly recommended for the wide benefits it brings to the site-seer, as well as to the organisations themselves much of whose important work must be funded out of earned income derived from the sites in their care. Full details of membership fees and privileges may be obtained at site offices throughout Great Britain.

The excellent Ordnance Survey Landranger maps are widely available and are indispensible to the serious traveller, particularly in locating those more remote sites that feature in the Traveller's Guide series. Their references and National Grid coordinates accompany each site entry.